SEAGULLS
&
SONNETS

by
CYNTHIA LUCY STEPHENS

ISBN 978-0-9955420-3-7

CIP record for this book

Cynthia Stephens
27 Retreat Crescent, Dunbar
E Lothian EH42 1GW Scotland UK
01368864354 / 07876177989
stephens.cynthia@gmail.com
cynthzzz@yahoo.com

Much love,
Cynthia

Seagulls & Sonnets

by

Cynthia Lucy Stephens

Cynth-by-Sea
Dunbar
Scotland
2020

Twitter: @CynthStephens

CONTENTS

Cynthia Lucy Stephens was born in Edinburgh and grew up in East Lothian. Much of her childhood was spent swimming in the sea and riding on horseback. Later she studied English and Spanish at Newcastle University, then went to live in Toledo, Spain, where she taught English. After a research degree at Cambridge University she published articles about the writer Jorge Luis Borges.

Having spent thirty years away
she returned to Scotland, where she worked for ten years as a Spanish translator from her seaside home in Dunbar. She has not been on a horse for over four decades, but she swam in the sea last summer.

BEGINNINGS

Horizons

Cynth they call me,
since I was born.
I was christened Cynthia -
the robe was white and long.

The church was Whitekirk,
Suffragettes burnt it.
I walked there through woods,
past burn. We worshipped.

In the arc of the moon,
the ships pass the Bass.
At the wink of our eyes,
lives ebb, tears shed.

Woman, your voice heard
the moon on your face.
Be still, find peace now,
the music of place.

The arc of your journey
from the hymns of the sea.
Like mermaids made human,
glory at your new horizons.

Beyond the yellow broom

Look! Yellow broom and blue sky; larks above,
singing joy, quivering on an arc of love.
Their little wings so delicate and light
are fragile, but their song is diamond bright.

Beyond the broom I see the estuary;
the river Tyne, and North Sea, precisely.
Around the curve of the bay lies the Bass;
with giant birds gobbling fish, solan geese.

It shines in the sunlight, white as ice-cream;
its guano and gannets a silver day-dream.
Its arc is wide, its embrace delicate.
It breeds ideas; it's iconic. Look!

Yellow broom and larks above:
this is all I know of love!
The Bass Rock and the booming sea:
this I know of eternity!

With Ice, Methinks

North Berwick, my first pool, and swimming wide
through icy water, adventure, enthralled.
To Fidra, Bass, the Craig, and Emerald
Isles, boating, paddling, great outdoors astride.

North Berwick, wind sharp, faces frozen, cold.
Its law so steep, our breath in gusts. Like sheep
on hillside, sheltering, we huddle, deep
in snow, mid-winter sun bright, blowing gold.

North Berwick, our ice lollies, fair ground rides,
and fun, great fun, as we were children then,
and all was jolly; dodgem cars; who hides,
who seeks? Or who has been into my den?
Yet now we still enjoy hot chocolate drinks
and warming things, like whisky, gin, methinks.

Beating the Waves

Six babies sitting on the sand,
two older ones hold their hands.
The Bass Rock regal out at sea,
the sky azure, like Tuscany.

The Car Rock jutting, pointing out
to meet the blue deep sea or sky.
A ladder on its tip, its steps
for climbing high to beat the waves.

These little babes are gurgling on the sand.
Their mothers watch them play and taste
the salt, where generations past
have crawled, and swum around these rocks.

I see my grandson play in the sand.
My father's mother holds the ladder.
She leads him by the hand.

Our Crucible, Our Cradle

The decades vanish at Ravensheugh,
St. Baldreds Cradle, my childhood crucible.
Below the cliffs the waters boom,
Around me now the sea pinks bloom.

Memory, my treasured landscape,
Your hand in mine my mind it takes.
Behind, where the horses ran, Belhaven Bay,
Ahead, vast gannet crag, the Bass.
On the far horizon I see the May Island,
Along the coast is Scoughall.
Westward lies Whitekirk still,
The church, the weddings, the hill.
But in between is the place where I dream,
Lochhouses, home, Elysium.
It is close, on my mind's horizon.

The wind blows, the sea air bites,
Make haste sister and brother.
Ride fast, for mother is warming the broth,
And father is in from the farm at last.
Come in from the windy cliff-top crag,
Where the wild sea pinks bloom,
Return now to our communal table,
Lochhouses, our birthplace,
Our crucible, our cradle,
For the horses are hurrying home.

The Family Face

"I AM the family face;
Flesh perishes, I live on."
Thomas Hardy

The genes slip down the generations,
they skip and skim like signals.
Like spirits with features,
their definitions reach us,
former lives in their traces,
forgotten people in their faces.

Three generations grace
this photo which ensures,
Jesse, Mary, baby Jean,
though the decades fade,
your look endures.

My daughter, Lucy,
looks out from the picture,
her face in the face, like a mirror,
of Mary, the mother,
who was married,
in nineteen nineteen.

Is she the same or is she another?
With the grace of my daughter,
she's her own great grandmother.
Down the generations the genes skip,
the family face remains, the spirit persists.

Winterfield

In January I pause
by the surging sea,
where concrete cubes merge
with the rocks.
Vast blocks, to preserve us
from war, they hide us.
Anti-Nazi devices,
washed where I walked,
as a child by the waves.

What fiancés were lost
in earlier French fields?
What mistress misery was felt,
what lonely agony?
A generation of women,
bereft in February.

Two teachers not mothers,
we were their children.
Eternal, the ebb and flow,
eternal, the debt I owe them.
The web of words we spelled,
the waft of silk thread we sewed,
in my first school by the sea.

Fifty years have come and gone,
the cubes of concrete are still strong.
They kept the enemy out,
and saved our generation.

For my teachers' generation,
and for their agony,
in the wild winter winds,
where the sea-weed webs its way,
so far from spring clover,
I feel peace, but I crave their pardon.
Here, on this beach,
not Dover, but Belhaven.

Mid-Winter Stars

We trudged through snow, our wellies deep;
our sledges shot down hills at speed.
Our snow-balls crisp, we threw and ran;
our laughter crackling in the air.
Above our heads the Pole Star shone;
it's light our guide to urge us on.

We sang of Good King Wenceslas,
who trod through pristine snow.
A winter hare went racing past,
A reindeer jumped the holly.

Thick ice was on the water trough;
the horses neighed; the cattle mooed;
we smashed the ice so they could drink.
The bleak mid-winter cracked our skin;
it bit our fingers, toes, and nose.
But we rejoiced. Our wondrous world!

The logs were crackling; fire was full.
We posted letters, to North Pole,
to Santa Clause, and reindeers too.
"Please bring me, with the jingle bells,
my favourite toy, a polar bear."

But now I hear there is no snow.
The sleigh is in the shed, the pole
is flooded. Reindeer have retired.
In Ursa Minor, night-time sky,
the polar bears are frozen stars.

Sometimes

Sometimes I like to eat toast,
hot and buttered, by the fire.
Crystal eyes burn red hot,
through smouldering logs.
Outside the frost bites the air.
Thoughts crystallize in warm embers.

Sometimes we like to lie down
on the Lammermuirs,
hills purple as plum jam,
heather our feather-down.
There are flowers on the ridge;
a bird with bright plumage trills;

Sometimes my grandmother knits,
row by row, stitch by stitch.
Her needle will track and trace
more lines than her face.
Knit one, purl one. Let the wool
that covered the lamb be fine.

Sometimes a dog lies curled,
a foetus, the couch a womb.
He does not bark, he does not whimper.
His thoughts just tumble and whirl,
rushing a cat, crouched by a tomb.
Let sleep knit up his sleeve of care.

Sometimes a blanket of frost will cover the hills.
Sometimes a blanket of flowers will cover the ridge.
Sometimes a blanket of wool will keep out the chill.
Sometimes a blanket of sleep will save us from harm.

"Vertumnus" by Arcimboldo

"In the sweat of thy face shalt thou eat bread,
till thou return unto the ground;" Genesis.

A Harvest Festival of a face. Your hair of pears and grapes.
With pea pod eyelids and pear nose, corn in your hair
and a ring of roses. Above carrot carbuncles your eyes are hollow.
Your crown of grain hints at pain, the eternal return, the inevitable cycle.
Bread to ground to grain.

A Harvest Festival of memory, a Kirk with kith and kin.
Each brings a contribution, a celebration of harvest in.
One brings a sheath of corn, potatoes, leeks and onions.
A child brings strawberries in. Her mother flowers and honey
to Whitekirk brings .

A Harvest Festival Kirn,
the Gay Gordons to the accordion.
Strip the Willow left the barn shaking,
the Eightsome Reels a feast of dancing.
For those who had worked with the sweat of their face
to bring in the corn, to stack the bales, where children played,
all summer long, in the harvest house, labyrinthine home.
For young and old, for sick and well, and those who cooked and cared,
bread was broken, thanks was given, a glass was filled, a living Heaven,
Auldhame was its name.

Now it is "Auld Lang Syne".
We took that "cup o' kindness".
Far from our minds that the kirn would die,
we crossed our hands and sang, in fond farewell,
and thought, "Should auld acquaintance be forgot?"
The Kirk is empty too, save the grave to the side,
where mother and father now abide.
And I will sometime too.

Vertumnus, your Harvest Crown will soon be changed, will be transformed.
An alchemical compound returns to the ground.
The hollow of your eyes will metamorphose, your crown will turn to thorns.
But this child who played, all summer long, in a labyrinthine harvest home,
will remember you, auld acquaintance.
Long after you have gone.

Gutted

A clifftop by the Bass, a shear drop,
the sea below. A monastery here;
the bones still lie. So many centuries
ago, the dead were laid at Auldhame.

The gulls fly high above the Ghegan Rock
or hunt for worms among the graves.
Millennia flit and flutter by, a breath
of time, like feathers, guano, foam on waves.

Below the graveyard lies a quarry, strata,
years in layers. Some little tents are pitched.
Teenagers flit about, their fire is lit,
and eggs are being fried. Aromas float
through time. And now I see my cousin smile,
a wide grin, laughing. Fish in hand, and knife.

Newhouse

The distant Paps of Fife are capped with snow.
The Firth of Forth is visible nearby.
All white and shiny, Fidra lighthouse close.
An old farm-house, with cottages, one row.

We walk the hill, our downward route, with ease.
To East lies Highfield, Berwick Law, the sea.
We turn the corner, in the farm itself,
the sign says NEWHOUSE, here by the old house.

The sun is high, the sky blue, choices
in the air. The sign NEWHOUSE, a weathercock
above is pointing North, East, South and West.
A baby in the garden, her pram rocking
to and fro, the sea breeze cradling her.
Tall trees shading her, here is my mother.

Whale's Teeth and Whorls

In Skara Brae the children play, the beach
has silver sand, grey pebbles, slabs of stone.
Their village close, its passages their home.
It's summer; blue skies, butter cups, and boats.

At Skara Brae the wind-swept bay is dark.
Tonight the stars cannot be seen. They hide
behind the clouds of winter. Puffs of smoke
arise from stones, a sign of life on earth.

In Skara Brae the children huddle round
the fire within their home, their parents near.
The night is dark, the winter vicious, daylight
precious, stories born from sea and storm.

Whale's teeth and whorls for toys. An eyebrow sketch
on bone. A star is drawn, lozenge on stone.

North

We leave Aberdeen, the compass points northwards,
the ferry heads towards our Nordic past.
At Sumburgh Head a lighthouse beacons at last,
ancestors lighting the long route homewards.

If I once heard the sound of buried reels,
Shetlandic tunes, a fiddle travelling,
Clickimin's Grand Dance, our old kirns replaying,
the Broch's stones would move to toes and heels.

My name is Dahl; I danced by the rounded broch.
By night dark peat glowed, a family home.
Our ponies are grazing beside the loch,
the wool is sheared and spun, our lambs have grown.

Precarious on the rocks like Lerwick seals,
I could hear the singing of Auld Hame reels.

The Tide is Out

Smell seaweed,
hear the waves,
taste the salt,
feel the cold,
see the sea.

Children shivering,
sea-breeze shimmering,
the water freezing,
hot chocolate awaiting,
our leaving.

Warm bodies
kissed by the sun.
We taste, we touch,
each one his own.
The sea is leaving.

The beach is bare,
a blank place
on which to run.
In our salty plans
we touch the sun.

The tide is out.
We wait a while.
When it draws close,
we will kiss its shimmering,
for we are leaving.

Bridge to Nowhere

Home is the sound of water.
Is it the North Sea,
or is it the River Cam,
on its bridge to the future?

Past is the sound of love now.
Is it the foetus to be,
or is it the mother,
home, with her face to the future?

Sea has the sound of the river.
Is it the summer surf,
or is it the winter,
sleet, on the bony ridge brow?

Home is the bridge to nowhere,
built at Belhaven Bay
on an eternal river,
that flows past, like my future.

IN BETWEEN

Photograph of Myself

Image, or mirage, imagine her past.
Cheeks that glow, smooth skin, bright lips, and closed eyes.
"Gather your rosebuds", said Herrick the wise,
for you will be gathered and cropped at last.

Moment of laughter, a camera snaps.
An instant is captured. Real or a pose?
Old photo, down decades of highs and lows,
that timeless smile has survived all mishaps.

Who is she, I wonder? I knew her once.
Some memories spark the feelings she knew.
Never dreaming her image beautiful,
her smile skipped the mirror and went on jaunts.
She's a digitized mirage, soft as dew.
In that decade rosebuds were plentiful.

Edinburgh Central Bus Lost Property Office

One Art, this life, more luck than art I sometimes say.
Others plan their lives. I don't.
'Cause I learnt early, that plans don't work.
So I lost a few dreams, then others emerged.
Surprises, unexpected, surging from the Zeitgeist, and the mix
that was me, at the time.

When the time is ripe.
Strange expression, as if time were an apricot, or a plum.
It can be.
But sometimes it is an acorn, small and mean, hard as nuts.
No squirrels even interested.

At other times it flows.
Not just a Heraclitus regret, but pulling us,
a dream of everlasting zoom.
Tiles on the pool surface curved, swimming.
Space-time even within our grasp.
Tectonic plates slip to our demand, the parabola of youth.
Dreams, where lost meant we would find.
Not star-fish washed up on the shore.

I lost my music-case so often on the buses.
About ten, a naive school-girl.
My mother made me go alone to the Bus Lost Property Office.
That was an early adventure.
Setting out on my own.
A pattern that recurred.

Entangled Like Brambles

Cold boarding school, by the North Sea,
me alone, no family.
(Sent there to learn to stand on my feet,
I learnt, and I went away.)
A rare visit, car journeys, round the rocky corner.
The Bass from Anstruther,
Turner's view. A distant family together,
entwined on the farms, like brambles.
For me, the sea, the waves, Virginia Woolf,
and the start of an eternal ride.
Exile, like autumn leaves turning red,
on the covers of books.

Queens Ferry

From South to North we cross. The ferry boats
are full. And we, as children run and jump,
enjoy the ride, the waves, the gulls, our throats
alive with laughter. Queen of hearts our trump.

From youth to age we ride the waves and foam.
The ferry boats have gone, they've been replaced.
A road bridge now will take us quickly from
the South to North. No salt, no sound, no taste.

Today we crossed the Forth, the river deep
below. Then on the North we felt the wind;
and in our hearts the sound of loss, the beat
of time, the drums, the years, the sins.
Under the shadow of the bridge, the Firth
still flows. And love, that Demon, last and first.

Darkness

A Scottish farmhouse, the 1950s.
Dead cold and dark of winter.
A thunderstorm and the lights went out.
My mother lit candles.
The silver candelabra glistens,
and the memory of love.

It's the 1970s.
Liberation of the Three Day Week.
Four days to explore, the uncharted unknown,
from dawn to dusk, or dusk to dawn.

Plunged into the Darkness,
power cuts adventure,
comradeship and candlelight.
Oblivious to parent's fears.

The economy in tatters,
a joyous gift to me.
Three days of typing quite enough
to finance four days free.

Six weeks I did in Barclays Bank,
London, Victoria. Typing 40 WPM.
Invite to a South London party
from the young friendly manager.

Two am, I am walking back home
in pitch black darkness, alone.
Through Brixton and across the river,
less boring than the banker's party.
A trip etched in my memory.

On the Border (1973)

In Mashhad we camped for a week.
I was afraid only of giant ants
that clambered constantly over limb and shank;
boredom broken by a bazaar sortie, where the hordes stared,
and I stoned their touch.
My head held high; my pretty face, I now know,
as I gaze at an old photo.
Claustrophobia, how they crowded, staring and invading my space.
I was in their space, that July.
Still unafraid, still unabashed; at twenty, who would be cowed?
And the stones that I threw were so small.

On my map, I look up Mashhad.
To the south "Plateau of Iran", to the east "Afghanistan".
South east, along the border, there lies Pakistan.
There went our cranky bus, through tribal lands of Baluchistan,
through deserts, dirt track, and war.

At Quetta they watched us with guns;
without water we waited, and waited.
What crisis was this we had stumbled upon?
The World Service was guiding us on.
With a skin of gooseflesh, and bowels of water,
the first fear drew near, like a noose of slaughter.
I had crossed a new border.
Now August, I had changed and was older.

More than three decades on,
I gaze at a photo of a girl who is young.
Wonder if she was me!
I remember the hordes, as they watched and touched.
I fear for the girl on her border.
I'm invisible now, free to see, only see.
And it seems a wild dream, a Surreal imagining,
to have crossed the tribal lands of Baluchistan,
ignorant of map or politician,
free of defence or weapon,
with just youth, and its beauty and joy,
and its fearless, innocent expression.

Toledo

Rock city,
Navel of the Peninsula,
circled by the Tagus
your beauty amazes.

Rock city,
El Greco knew you.
Your darkness and light
were both in his View.

Rock city.
At Corpus Christi they come
for the floral carpets
and the hair shirts of the penitent.

Rock city.
The Inquisition is in the air,
the "hostia" rises,
as the hags scream for vengeance.

Rock city.
Francisco Franco thanked you
for fearing no bombs or Republicans.
Your Alcazar was strong.

Rock city,
Heart of the Peninsula,
through the veins of the Tagus
have flowed many ages.

Rock city.
I lived and loved in you,
and there I left a piece of my heart
and I hear it beat still.

Rock city.
I listen still for the layers
of history, of meaning, as they linger
in my Navel and that of the Peninsula.

Rock city,
I pursue my lost youth
in your ancient stones,
and the flowers and the sins that were my own.

"Christ's Cross and Adam's Tree"
after John Donne and Norman Adams.

The first garden beckons, flowers bright;
apples ripe, their taste so perfect, juicy.
Adam bites deep, and as he does so
the tree appears to lose its leaves, the birds
stop singing, the yellow sun hides.

Forgive us Lord for we have sinned.
Forgive our cowardice and pride.

The cross has formed upon the tree
and Christ is hanging from its boughs.
Pray, let us help caress his feet
and watch the light descend tonight.

So let the gallows creak and scream,
and let the birds return to nest,
and if the flowers of Paradise
should bloom again, then let the Heavens
spray colour on the world,
and link the boughs of then and now
with halos bright and new.

Air Whispers Through Vines

The Iron Duke
marched up the Tagus
to battle by the water.
The blood flowed faster
than wine, by the river.
In the words of the old song
"The Tagus is always young."

In Talavera de la Reina,
I saw the first wrinkle
curl around my eyes.
My skin like milk,
"como la leche", I was told,
by those with pigment like gold.

The golden sun burnt
in the summer furnace
and Spanish skin
was hardy like bronze.
The beauty, the warmth,
the hospitality,
almost took my breath away.

The Duke has long gone,
the river is not young.
The Tagus has been maimed,
transformed to a trickle.
The smooth running ore
the river of gold,
is now crumpled and old,
conquered and sold.

Gold to gold,
Iron to iron.
Haemoglobin fills lungs,
air whispers through vines.
The wine from a "bota"
makes blood flow faster.
A wrinkle round the eyes,
for sorrow or laughter.
A trickle of tears
the defeat of the river.

The Horns of a Dilemma

The Matador was handsome,
a bull's horns shone in the searing sun.
The crowed roared loud.
Fiesta fun had just begun.

Horn to the right,
Horn to the left.
Loud "Olés" in the air.
Swing the red cape.
Stay close. Don't Fear!

Choose:
Fame or disgrace.
Choose:
Life or lingering death.

On the horns of a dilemma
the Matador balances all.
He meets death, martyrdom, or shame.
Stacked up high, the losses, the gains.
Both sides of the line.

The bull bellows,
his breath is visible,
his whiskers, his eyes.
The two animals hold their gaze,
then a bell chimes.
Is it close by?
or high in the heavens?

It calls them both.
One of them must cross
that crimson line
where hot blood meets cold.
Stiff sinews of destiny.

Pinned to the ground or pinned to a wall.
Horns and sword, point right and left.
Upwards, then straight ahead.

Spanish Fragments

Córdoba, Salamanca, Santiago, Toledo.
I love you, Spain. I rode big night trains,
from Paris to Hendaye. Onto Madrid and Seville.
And little ones that stopped at every "pueblo".
Each tiny village a world.
Each new journey an adventure.

I loved you, Spain.
I knew you before democracy dawned,
while Fascism still stalked your streets and your jails.
On the overnight trains from Paris
the men were laughing, handsome, tactile, fun.
I froze in a "pensión" by the "Puerta del Sol",
The Gate of the Sun, the Centre.
The one "brasero" under a table
not enough to warm all our legs.
Madrid at New Year, the "copas" spinning,
my head in the clouds, at home with strangers.
Franco dead, the Old Year closing,
an era ebbing into oblivion.

I loved you, Córdoba.
In boiling summer on the banks of the Guadalquivir.
Dancing a drunken flamenco, castanets held high,
clip clopping to the beatings of our hearts.
The "siesta" a half-death necessity in 42 degrees.
Then cooling off with sweet wine in the "judería" bars.
Strolling back after midnight.
Medieval streets, Andalusian stars.

I loved you, Toledo.
Labyrinthine City on the snake of the Tajo.
The river looping its labyrinth.
The serpent biting its tail.
Figs picked in the gardens of "Cristo de la Luz" mosque.
Corpus Christi fragrance, rosemary and thyme.
Multiple jobs merrily juggled.
Lodgings matching the season.
In winter some heating, and hot water.
In spring a bathroom view, Cathedral,
and kittens coming in from the rooftops.
A view of the "Cigarrales".
And stars over the "meseta".

Barcelona, Nerja, La Coruña.
I loved your coast. Oh Spain!
Toasting on your golden beaches with friends.
Dear Lorna, now gone, in Nerja.
María, old pal, in Torredembarra.
Cats and naked artistry in Sitges.
"Playa de las Americas", Tenerife.

Spain.
I loved your mountains.
Monserrat,
its monastery a jewel rising over the clouds.
Its black virgin adored by pilgrims.
Beauty cloaked in sadness and loss.
Mount Teide,
where we clambered over volcanic pathways
near the top of the world's spout.
Air crisp but thin.
Avila,
a long train journey from Madrid, ascending.
Upwards again to the Celtic hill forts
in an old friend's four by four.
A discussion of grammar.
Past simple or preterite?
Different names for completed actions.
I see a statue of Santa Teresa, as I descend,
remember her Dark Night of the Soul.
Is the past ever simple I wonder.

Spain.
I knew you before the EU opened its doors.
Before it shone its yellow stars on you.

Spain.
I am afraid I will lose you.
I fear you will fragment,
become a figment of my memory.
One golden star burning.

Sun on the Giralda

Oranges and Lemons
save the joys of the Heavens.
When will we pick them,
asked the gardener from Seville.
When the tourists flow freely
down the Guadalquivir.

In the shadow of the Giralda,
the oranges are golden,
their sweet juice a feast,
each segment a dream.
From the high tower of Seville,
you see Cordoba's river.
Follow back the dark water,
where the olive trees grow.
Far away from the river,
from the songs and the voices,
another language rules,
which is harsh and so cruel.

At five in the morning the blow fell,
at five in the morning exactly.
The dogs barked
and the cicadas shrieked
in the warm warm air.
The smell of the lemon trees
hung bitter there,
suffused with the taste of fear.

At five in the morning exactly
I ate a bitter olive.
There was no white sheet, no.

Oranges and Lemons
sweet joy of the Heavens!

A Mountain to Climb

My brother was a climber.
I preferred books.
My brother liked potholes.
I liked pubs.

When I was sixteen
I skied the Cairngorms.
My face swelled up in a blizzard.
I was sent back home.

I skied at Davos
with granny and sister.
Slopes so steep.
Horse sleighs in the streets.

When I was fifty four
I crossed the Andes
on buses and boat.
Conac, hot chocolate, catamarans.

The mountain air of Bariloche,
was crisp and clear.
A Nazi paradise in former years.
We saw Lago Nahuel Huapi from up high.

At Sugarloaf we saw the fog
and mountain trinkets in the shops.
The cable car went up and down
keeping tourist schedules sweet.

In Tenerife the volcano spouts.
Teide sends its smoke signals out.
Some like to climb up,
some scramble down.
We went up in a mechanical pod.
I offered a loan of my coat at the top.

Some people do not know
high points are so cold.
I adore the top of a mountain.
Hot chocolate in the shieling, even more.

Blue Skies at the Crater

No snow on the Teide volcano.
No water in the "estanque".
The rains have not come to Tenerife.
The sun shines on, no mercy.

No snow on the Teide volcano,
but we ascend nevertheless.
A sordid scrum at the bus stop.
An asthma puffer tucked in my pocket.

No snow on the Teide volcano.
The cable car swings and sways.
A view of Mars perhaps
would seem less fierce and strange.

No snow on the Teide volcano.
No, and not much air.
So slowly, we step with care
on rubble paths of lava.

No snow on the Teide volcano,
but a puff of smoke at the crater.
So dormant today in the sun,
blue sky breathing, just like us.

Waiting

"The rite of the falling sand is infinite
and, with the sand, our lives are leaving us."
Alastair Reid, "The Hourglass", translated from Jorge Luis Borges.

I waited, more than twenty years to visit you.
Oh Buenos Aires,
Borges City.

I was waiting in Cambridge, when we went to war.
"Las Malvinas", our Falklands, some islands in the ocean.
You wrote in The Times: "Juan Lopez and John Ward".
I watched the navy each night, to see if my brother-in-law
had died.

After the war my baby was born.
It seemed that from your books she had flown.
Breast feeding I read your Seven Nights,
in Spanish, on a stand, in our flat, with the walls falling down.
I was weaving my own labyrinth of words
from your words, and though those tigers of symbols exist
in the great libraries of the world, I see them through a glass darkly.
What remains is a marriage, a baby, a great university,
a memory of meeting you, who we had dinner with,
so blind and gentle like a myth.

Last night, another ancient man who has known you,
and whose words have united you two, as in one author,
the maker, the poet, the creator,
signed his book in Edinburgh,
for Cynthia with Pleasure.

Edinburgh, Cambridge, Buenos Aires.
Borges knew them all,
but chose instead to die in Geneva,
where different memories grew.

Buenos Aires,
I waited so long to know you
that Borges had gone,
the glass had turned,
the hours had flown,
the sand had moved on.
In the master's words:
"con la arena se nos va la vida".
Only words remain
where the Immortals reign.

Metempsychosis

The travelling soul,
is saddened, transposed.
A young self returned
to a mid-life mind,
a past future burned
on a pyre out of time.
The power of a paragraph,
translated, transformed,
from the hours of oblivion,
buried words reborn.
My name is late
on the parchment of fame,
ideas immortal
in the writers' game.

Baby on a Bicycle

The Cam flows gently by Jesus Green lock.
One barge is an art gallery at last.
A baby on a bicycle rides past.
The wheels have turned like the hands of my clock.
The Cam flows softly, Grantchester Meadows.
The punts move calmly, young couples at ease,
deck-chairs, the apple orchard, cakes and teas.
And honey, of course, this song will echo.
The bicycles ride by the towpath still,
from Magdalene Bridge to Stourbridge, the wheels turn.
My baby now an artist, a woman.
Her mother puffs out of breath on a hill.
The immortal Cam sings, memories burn.
But from ten to three, my clock has moved on.

Passing

I pass through the door, I'm in my old hall.
The mirror has still its crack on the wall.
Time waits, stands still, a labyrinth.

Years ago, Tinch grasped the brass
on the carpet floor, a flame of orange,
at the kitchen door, as Hanne beamed.

Passion flowers bloomed in purple and blue,
laughter, a Bar B Q. An hour-glass turned,
a garden torn, returned to sand.

I remember Hanne, her beauty and harmony,
in a dusty old photo, bright as the bride.
When marriages died, we both survived.

As a bank bit the dust, and Wall Street cracked,
a cathedral led me, a labyrinth, a maze of spirit.
In Norwich, I worshipped.

After the burial,
I wandered with Tinch through Tombland cathedral.
Together we wondered at the stone-built miracle,
and the flame of friendship.

It flared like her intellect,
her beam, a passion seed, a threshold of thought.
It leads us to the labyrinth, past the crack in the mirror
and the sand in the glass.

Time waits, stands still, as we pass.
Before us unfolds the unknown story
of another person.
A passing away,
where the spirit remains.

Goblet of Wine

Snug as a ring lies Fafnir,
dragon, feasting, drinking ale.
A lone minstrel, breath of fire,

sweetest sounds, a nightingale.
Crowded hall, goblet of wine,
the poet recites his tale.

Fire circle, centuries shine,
darkest nights, reddest dawnings,
eons loop and intertwine.

A lone woman stands and sings,
silky hair so long and blond.
Golden threaded music rings

down hidden decades long.
A young woman listening
picks up the gold threaded song.

Her breath sharp, eyes glistening,
running with the reel, she leapt,
just jumping, not listening.

Labyrinthine secrets kept,
in Sol and Luna, strange dreams,
all tangled up, as she slept.

An old woman wakes and leans
towards the light, so silver.
Her hair, threadbare, hope still gleams,

singing tales of the river.
Her reel unwinds, and then she screams,
"Hearts are burning in the fire".

"A bull's horn is born in the thread,
but snug as its ring lies Fafnir".
Then she fled from the Minotaur's Head.

A lone minstrel, breathing fire.
Goblet of wine. Slainte mhath!

A Bold Woman of Drama

There was a bold woman of drama.
Her hair all bunched up like a llama.
When she opened her mouth,
out came words, songs, and gold.
The roaring crowds
clapped like thunder.

'Tis an oath, spoke the elf.
"Tis a prayer, purred the puss.
'Tis a murmur, said the river.
'Tis a story, whirred the wind.

And the siren on the island
wore her necklaces of salt.
While the ice on the mountain
glinted seer eyes, north and south.

Gasping crowds clapped their thunder.
Clouds clasped their rain.
Dew drop necklaces sparkled silver.
Lightning flashes sparked a chain -
of words and swords, and songs of glory,
ancestors, aunties, and ancient times.
Dramatic, magnetic, eccentric, hypnotic,
a wild style told of joy to behold.

All action and drama and strange past antics,
childhoods lit from the limits of time,
we clap and we laugh, and we thunder applause,
for Jill, with her hair bundled up like a llama,
for Jill in Dunbar, with her house on the hill.

And we laugh and we clap
like the thunder of old,
for the Silver Street home
with a heart of gold.

Charlotte Square

The faces seem older each year.
Do young people not read any more?
I mean books.
Paper books, with covers, well illustrated,
where Cuba can become a Colonial facade
and Scotland a tartan column.

And who was Charlotte anyway?
I see a statue of Prince Albert.
We know who he was, a star in Victoria biops.
I spot an old friend, quite eminent now.
His wife greets me joyfully.
Memories skip down three decades to Liverpool 8
when the riots were still spoken of in hushed whispers.
And a recent pizza in trendy Dulwich.

Our choices are vast:
Poetry, politics, biography, science.
All within a small square
whose shed-like tents get bigger every year,
with some now sloping off
down George Street, to the Spark Theatre.

Muriel left Edinburgh, and left America, for Italy.
She finally settled in a house in the country
where she could travel mentally anywhere,
back to Edinburgh, on to Peckham Rye.
Or back to New York,
where she and Alastair Reid
shared memories of childhood
in that Calvinist country,
where some are chosen
as God's "crême de la crême"
and some, naive and young,
fall at the One O'clock Gun.

Homecoming

"Is it never dead, then,
that need of an Eden?
Alastair Reid.

Opening the wound
I revisit my childhood home.
There is smoke in my mother's kitchen,
and the clocks have all moved on.

The stove is warm, the kettle hot,
the budgie chatters still.
Chirping like others, oblivious
to what is going on.

The fleeting trip unhinges me,
so short and yet so strong.
That past Eden is inside me,
this trauma a wound
that weeps at dawn.

Incense in Spirals

Your soul is freed from mortal coil, and soars,
escapes a body, heavy; held you down
too long; so now you float on incense wings,
which spiral upwards making smoky rings

and bringing back your spirit from the past
to land in Edinburgh one night before
they shot John Lennon. Innocence no more.
Our Old World Reekie reeled, and music crashed.

Now jazz is calling you again to dance
in harmony with hill and wind, to laugh,
and gallop horses through the skies, your chance
to win the race, to gather round your friends
to watch you swim, your wide wild deep north sea.
Incense in spirals; innocence set free.

Peace

Peace, how many ways can I say you?
You come dropping slow, where rainbows flow.
You come stealing by, where day-dreams grow.
You're a constant goal, an inner shore,
a perfect companion, my punctual friend.

Though tidal waves break, and daily bread aches,
with pains and strains. Though our cross awaits
a long journeying, we hear the white horses neighing,
the old donkeys braying, the frothing foam spraying,
splashing and spluttering, uttering for ever and for ever.

So let's give it a chance,
the peace,
that passes all understanding.

Shadows

Eros transformed
on a hill of time,
where the Red Fox was shot,
the trees entwined.

Philia regained,
in a valley of shade.
At the Red Sun I sense
your shadow behind.

Diamonds on the Path

The train travels fast on the route backwards,
Dunbar, Edinburgh, Falkland Estate,
the Lawn Market.
Moments merge:
our arms are linked on the castle path;
four decades dip and dive
like gannets round the Bass.

Cascading through man-made structures
cutting deep into earth,
where hunters, both common and royal
stalked their prey:
lithe young animals more tasty
than stringy tough ones.

An old voice,
the same yet different,
sounds of water as they fall,
drops so beautiful in the sunlight,
perfect and innocent,
then gone for ever;
absorbing the vast chain of elements,
linking rings and parted atoms;
never to meet again;
or to meet again eternally,
shivering like diamonds,
which are, we believe,
for ever.

Fetch the Ferryman

Ferry 'cross the Channel.
We kissed on the boat,
ignoring the holiday crowd,
en route to France.
Just a few days married,
and no-where booked in Paris,
I wondered, should I change my name?
To become truly one with him.
The wind blew in our hair. The sun shone.
The photo remains the same.

Ferry 'cross the Mersey.
We danced on the boat,
with the Bank Holiday crowd
en route to New Brighton.
The Beatles welcoming us to L'Pool.
Lucy, aged four, and me,
dancing the night away.
Her father somewhere else that day.
New life, noisy, unreal, raucous,
the twist, wild, She loves you Yea Yea Yea.
Last week in St. Andrews already
a distant discrete tear away.

Ferry out of Lerwick.
The seals were crying on Sooth Mooth,
at the height of the waves.
I sent a text to Lucy,
as I swallowed the pill.
Just in case, just in case
I don't come home again.
Vomit in the ladies toilet.
I wretch. I remember other Ferries.
My life unfolds behind my eyes,
where sharp seal tears lurk.

The mirror ticks, it's six o'clock.
The sundial stops, it's ten past ten.
The shadow lengthens, the mirror cracks.
Ice opens its hands, and grasps our toes.

The ferryman lingers, the river flows.
The fee is due, for follies past.
The ghosts are ashen, waiting near.
The mirror cracks, becomes broken glass.

Fetch the Ferryman. Fetch our Double.
Ferry again across the Channel!

Eavesdropping on Thomas Browne in the Seventeenth Century

From Cheapside and St. Paul's, his father merchant
of silk, his boyhood buzzed with trade and church,
Paul's Cross the centre, Cyrus Garden later.
From there he roamed, flowers, fields, the Thames.

His father dead, an orphaned boy, the world
showed him its Vulgar Errors and disease.
He studied medicine - Padua, Leiden.
Lessons in Anatomy, theatre of mankind.

Religio Medici, one of his miracles,
went straight to Latin, a lightning translation.
Around the continent it spun, his inner being
a quick sensation. Conversation, intimate.

Embryon Philosophers

Urn to "amphora", Browne to Borges.
Womb to tomb, our lives are doomed.
Lover of languages, diggers of dreams.
Syntactical trowels, gardens of prose.

Rhombic patterns, new worlds emerge.
Embryon ideas, struggle through birth.
Screams of pain, civil wars disperse.
Translation's game, time's migration.

Soul to soul, salt from earth.
An urn for burial, embryon for birth.

Mary A
In Memoriam

Mary, my friend,
"Madame Chapeau",
"Lady of the Hats".
How I miss you.

Your house like a museum,
but always the cracks
for your friends to climb through.

Your mind like a library,
histories, dynasties, family scandals.
All was grist to your mill.

Samuel Pepys
with his sister waiting at table,
a servant sibling.
His secret diary.

Your walk, basket on arm,
magnificent hat brimming with brio,
along the Backs.
Entering institutions by every door,
the floor above and the floor below.

Not too grand a lady to grace
my Bohemian Barbecues.
And later, much later,
let me sleep in your loft.

Rest now Mary,
in your grave in the sky.
Your spirit will stroll
with Pepys across Magdalene Bridge.
You are wearing a hat
from the distant Empire.
I see you swanning into "Raffles",
to interview Princes.

By the Bridge of Sighs and Songs

Silicon wrought from a Fen island,
a brief history, a line in time.
Medieval market, Stourbridge fair,
circle of friends, a scholarly venture.
That adventure by the Cam river,
a University, its time-line richer.
A universe of stars, some bright,
some scarcely visible in the night,
all valuable, with various virtues, fired.

By the Bridge of Sighs, they kissed,
by the Mathematical Bridge, they multiplied.
DNA was sequenced, philosophy transformed,
the principals of mathematics exposed.
Enigmas were cracked and codes discovered,
pulsating stars shone, astronomical miracles.

Scholar stars became legends,
names flare and then fade.
Erasmus' Renaissance and Newton's physics,
Darwin's evolution and Keynes' economics,
Wittgenstein, philosophy, Clerk Maxwell, electricity,
Russell, maths, and Hawking, that brief history.
Multiform faces, so many facets,
the line forms then dissolves and vanishes.
Even poetry has multiple laureates:
Tennyson mourns, "In Memoriam",
in "Lycidas" Milton grieves.
Together they teach us to remember.

A universe of the mind was mapped,
the lines on the page wrought tears.
Scholars shone, in deeds, in writings, in song.
We celebrate them on and on.
But I grieve also, for dead friends,
from my own circle, "In Memoriam" .
I grieve, but also celebrate,
those loved ones who have gone.
They rejoin a line of time which dissolves,
of minds and hearts, brief and bright.
Now eclipsed, but well remembered.

There in March

Thirty years of walking by Magdalene Bridge.
1980, an interview, with a college to follow.
1981, a wedding party, joyous to the eating.
1983 a baby, to be called, like me, Lucy.
1985 a degree, then for a while, away.
1989 and I'm working, 1994, writing.
Then divorcing, commuting.
Still walking, still cycling,
by the Magdalene Bridge.

"Time Warp on the Cambridge Backs" wafts me back,
in dreams, where I seem to see Samuel Pepys reveal his soul.
Time weaves its own mysteries, but the water still flows
under Magdalene Bridge.
And there in March the crocuses grow.

Library of Dreams

Edinburgh, Dublin, Buenos Aires:
one memorious day.

A blind man writing,
his white stick a guide.
Joyce follows Ulysses
through Dublin's long minutes,
Borges close behind,
tap tapping on the glass.

One quick glance in the mirror,
then the rhythm of the waves, lapping.
Is it Blind Pew who is tapping
or Odysseus' returning?

The voyager comes home
to the longed for hearth.
The blind reader dreams
in a library at last.

Portrait of the Artist

In Newcastle I turned the pages.
Through Dublin and Madrid
I roamed.
Say yes, I believed,
say yes,
to danger, ambition, desire.
Penelope's role not for me,
to sit and to wait and to weave.
I would rather risk all,
on one damn crazy fall
than be drawn for eternity.

Well, Ulysses he moved the waves
and heard the songs the Sirens sang.
I also heard some strange sweet tunes
from lips of strangers
turned to friends.

On the day I come back home
who will be waiting and weaving for me?
My cat would have purred,
I am sure,
but he left for the distant shore.
My pony would neigh,
hey hey,
but she rejoined her rowan tree.
Then when autumn came she was gone,
once more to the sea,
transformed from chestnut to grey,
then white as the foam on a winter's day.
There, is where I will be,
yet another portrait
born to live in the artist's eye.
White as light,
and fragile as a mirage.

Footsteps in the Mind

Dublin, more legend than real to me.
City on the Liffy, with Stiffy skywards,
a needle pointing, silver centre catching the sun,
where crowds gathered once, Heaven bound.

We walk with books, long lost ghosts of words.
A life-like statue of George Bernard Shaw
welcomes me at the National Gallery,
and Joyce is lurking in St. Stephens Green.

A Harp Bridge spans the river;
its chords of steel seem to hold the city
tight in a clasp of music and strength,
as banks and hi-tec dance with Temple Bar.
Trinity College, grand like Cambridge,
where once the footsteps of genius echoed,
of Swift, Beckett, and Boyle;
where the voice of a gentle friend of mine,
can be heard, close by, in conversation still.

The Last Peninsula

A jagged giant lying in the ocean,
slain by glaciers, watching the stars.
Around him are sharks, and gulls a-plenty.
The Blasket Islands, westwards all empty.

At Sybil Point predictions whisper;
crones in the waves, their arrows chatter.
Needle-sharp their loss, and memories;
the mountains sheer; future unclear.

Westward migration, where famine flies.
There destiny sailed; the past had sunk.
A friendly dolphin, sun on the sea,
brings the present to fore, sets the Sybil free.

Beehive houses abuzz with tourists,
bus tours zigzag the road on the edge.
Still the lambs frolic on Dingle grass,
but the giant rock can sunbathe at last.

Maps Are So Much Prettier Today

A colour for each region, Ireland. Green
where Galway lies, the west; orange for Cork;
then Dublin red, where Bloom's James Joyce is seen
North of the Liffy; "Ulysses" his work.

The bright North West has Yeats' Sligo, Ben
Bulben, and Isle of Innisfree, "I will
arise and go now". Belfast, now and then,
Giant's Causeway, sea, turquoise still.

The roads are coloured too. The motorways
are blue. And ferry ports have little boats;
an icon makes it clear. We plan our days,
our routes; we navigate this island, books
our guide, their glossy pictures; smart-phone app.
So much prettier than the other map.

A Meditation in the Bath *

My Inspiration will not come, I fear
a Trout has blocked my Pipes. The Bath is full,
the Water will not flow. Oh Doctor, hear
me Please, this Block is Personal, not cool.

My Gurgling Thoughts are slipping out of reach,
their Silent Waves are Safe, they harm no-one.
They're happy down the Plughole, each with each.
No Dialogue of Words, no Chat, begun.

So Doctor, Doctor, may I call you Quack?
If Ducks may make this Sound, and thus Discourse,
so foolishly, then why not we? We who
have Minutes, Guidelines, Conduct, Codes. One Whack!
My Pen, my Stick, would hit the Mark, of course.
My Silent Block, no danger there. Hey Ho!

* Inspired by dipping into Swift's "Tale of a Tub"

Miles Away

My train time flickers on and off the board.
I examine it carefully, there's time
for lager, the 'Nor Loch, music wonderful,
the drunks quite out of line tonight, no doubt.

The Belfast child still sings again, then once
upon a time, Bob Dylan sings, oh how,
how does it feel, a rolling stone, no moss,
it gathers none, just rhythm sound and pace.

I examine the TV, Will and Kate,
then Charles, Camilla - Diana dead -
and Dylan sings on, blowing in the wind,
his voice the message, too many have died.

Examining my mobile, time to go
inside, outside, I see for miles and miles!

Miles and Miles in Context

Five thirty. Too little sleep. Not in bed 'til one.
What with late night news, Libya, Japan,
combined with LinkedIn, automatic mailings.
A good breakfast to start a good day.
Loch Katrine from the first train
then coach then fry up on the square.
Five pm whirl on the bike in a hurricane.
Belhaven Bay.
A can of larger, with a whisky thrown in,
just to put the day in context.
Another great day!

Melting the Light

A festive sun of honeyed wax,
hexagonal and sharp its lens.
A bee has flown then falls the axe

on golden corn which breaks, which bends.
The buzz of summer festivals,
he neither heeds nor comprehends.

And pollen wings his duty calls,
a golden powder cloaks his flight.
A drone, a queen? A princess falls.

A shower of gold, a God, in sight.
A flash from Zeus melts the light.

The Golden Corn

I wish that the summer would remember
when it goes down the hill in the west,
that January's ahead of November,
and the earth holds new seeds in its breast.

I wish summer beach days were longer,
when tides pull back and hot sand is yellow.
Rock pools a mirage of earlier summers;
fish-nets in hand. New children; Hello!

I wish for summer barns full of ripe grain,
cygnets, chicks, goslings, feathered and old,
seasons cycling round, again and again.
I wish golden corn should not turn to gold.

Historical

Ghosts come roaming across the Border
to linger awhile on the Royal Mile.
To play as statues, like David Hume,
static, historic, made of stone.

Amazing the Crowds

Am I a clown
or a jumping bear?
They're clapping louder,
through the smoke I hear.
They shout my name
out, Cyn, or Sin, my fame
is monstrous, ridiculous,
flying in the face of decorum.

And where is the poem?
It is lost in the jeers
of more labyrinths, more high jumps,
all laughs and jokes, no tears,
a veritable olympics of verse.

So terse, so bizarre,
so biting, such guitar.
Am I the jumping clown or the laughing bear?
Tonight we will see
if the audience is three,
or three hundred, a trinity
of one, two, three, you and me,
plus zero, zero,
for the hoops we leap through.

Leap higher, jump smarter,
imagine sharper, and you too can be
that amazing jumping bear!

The Devil Dances Samba

All that jazz, all that samba.
We kick our feet, we click castanets.
The music drums and the rhythm beats,
click clock, click clock.

Or hearts tick slower and slower,
our pulse throbs weaker and weaker.
We are older each summer,
clip clop, clip clop.

The Free Fringe summons us
to fly in the face of common sense,
to click the strings, and lick the gravy,
from supper rich with wine and honey.

So its money, buzzing, booze and blindness,
the Bible collides with popular ballads.
Madonnas and motherhood alive in the suburbs,
Devils dance samba, but not in Prada.

"To everything there is a season",
So keep to the special samba rhythm.
The grim reaper is watching,
love and the dance wait not.
Tick tock, tick tock.

Sciatica

My nerves are jangling
like a jack-in-the-box.
I jump.
A disc injury,
a temporary disability?
Muscles are wasting
with this waiting, waiting, waiting.
A tortoise plodding
for hours through mud.

I want to race like a hare
but I judder and thud.
I aspire like Zeno,
to infinity's jeers.
Stranded in slime,
wrecked by time,
a turtle bound
to go round and round.

The clock hands tick,
clickety click.
The hip bone bites
as the nerve ends tighten.
Move slowly Jack,
do not jump,
or the box will shut
and the hour will strike.

Open it slowly,
springs and locks.
Ease yourself gently
like the hands of a clock.
Tick tock, tick tock.
All those days lost.
Lost in these thoughts.

Dance On

What goes around then comes around.
So go along and come back soon.
Quick step you gaily, up and down.
Skip pas de basque, and paws on bums.

The legs will lead, then heads will swoon.
The arms will welcome, squeeze you too.
A lady's chain will capture you,
enraptured in a thought balloon.

Even Dilbert dances, be it known:
Release him now from worker groans.
Before the beast within bursts out,
Before the dance begins let's shout:

Quick step you gaily, in and out,
Dance on, move in, move out, red hot!

The Wheels of Thought

What goes round, comes around, about.
The wheels are whizzing faster, faster, back.
The reels we're dancing, heels, toes, running track.
Those leaps of faith are morphing late to doubt.

From disco dance to stranger's bed one night.
Adventure grasped, a thistle held in hand.
A purple flower that bloomed, a door that slammed.
What was so real has now been lost from sight.

A London bed, soft mattress with a spike.
A slap that woke me sharply from my trance.
So tall, so handsome, gentle most, he taught
me not to trust, to run, to get my bike;
to keep the photos but rejoin the dance.
The pricks that hurt have now become mere thought.

The Bacchus House

The drunken world staggers and falls,
walking wounded cram our hospitals.
The sirens sound, the walls crash,
ambulances, emergencies, the wounds gash.

Wall street has spoken,
the beast has awoken.
"Six six six" I hear him called.
All that glitters is not gold.

With her empty eyes and naked claws,
"Witch witch witch" I hear her called.
She ripped his entrails out as she stripped.
She whipped the cat as she grabbed a drink.

Caravaggio's Bacchus, so serene,
inspiration and divination a strange dream.
The wine and the song have given way
to lewd lyrics and wild ecstasy.
Boundaries crash down,
and souls are trampled on.

A drunk woman humming,
a small child running,
raucous Bacchus is back in his house.
Delicious delirium, domestic war,
the drunken house tumbles,
it staggers and falls.

Round Robin

Ring a ring of roses,
the world is round.
A pocket full of posies,
we all fall down.

Ring a ring of money,
the tills of the world are full.
The dollars turn to Euros,
the yens are spinning too.

Electronic currency,
bits and bytes of commerce.
They spin and ring, out of control.
We run and dodge the bullets.

The army moves,
the air-force too.
Old kit bags fly back,
flanked by flags.

The chartered flights
fly to and fro.
Travel and tourism,
the thing to do.

The travel routes thrive,
the child is young.
So many miles
to see the first-born.

Grandmother pines,
grandfather aches.
Was it all for this,
we struggled and strained?

The Robin still sings
by the old window sill.
Will my grandchildren hear him?
Will he sing for them still?

Ring a ring of roses,
the world is still round.
But do video links and telephones
raise us up, or knock us down?

Honey Money

Pounds, euros, dollars,
yens, cents or dimes.
We don't discriminate.
Your dosh we can integrate.
Cash, cheques and transfers,
or payment in kind.

How will you earn it,
borrow, beg or steal it?
Drive a bus, or business,
shoot a rabbit, set a budget?
The colour of your money
is irrelevant. Like honey,
if it's sweet we love it.

The bees are buzzing round the pot.
The workers work, the others not.
The structure of the hive is such
that each bee occupies its slot.
The queen is sucking out some honey,
stolen from the royal factory.
But the king is in his board room,
eating cake and counting money.

Confessions on the Cowgate

Another day of Royal Mile flyering.
Our show is squashed between Old Jewish Jokes
and Heavy Petting. Laughter almost chokes
on chicken wings; to fly is so tiring.

Led Zeppelin in the ladies is the best,
and Star of Wonder lager, just say Star
O, yes, and old friends landing from afar;
our raucous laughter heals, I do not jest.

Our gig's in Blackfriars Street, a Bar, CowGate
close by, where cattle entered town, and friars
prayed, and preached, Aquinus their dear late
brother. Confessions, sins, truth-tellers, liars.
In cities centuries ago, old slums,
our tales were told. Now poetry, music, drums!

Croaking to the Show

The raven croaks, the lark sings high and low,
The Black Death stalks me, Blackfriars Street its show.
My spirit high, my voice below, hey ho!
What fatal entrance, mercy I implore.

Story

How does it begin?
With chickens,
On the wing.

Where is the middle?
Clucking, laying, pecking.
Feathers, fear and muddle
as a fox bursts in.

And the end?
An attempt to fly
with birds soaring like words
above foxes and pig sties,
where no-one lives and no-one dies.
A history of truths and lies.

All the World's a Stage

"Which circus do you act in?" asked the clown.
"Where no-one has a name", replied the king.
"Your daughter loves you like no living thing."
"Her laughter makes me shiver and lie down."

The circus animals are begging for a coin.
The blind man and the fool are waiting in the wing.
The woman with a throat infection stands to sing.
The gladiator hesitates then girds his loins.

The stage is set for everyone.
One entrance; just one exit.
The circus may be short or long.
Your role may range from infant to oblivion.
You can embrace it or reject it.
A weak performance, or better strong.

The Trapeze Artist's Song

"Which circus do you act in?" asked the clown.
The acrobat was flying through the air.
Swooping down she spiralled without a care
"Where cocks are crowing but the notes are wrong."

The trapeze artist, flying through the air,
while faces below, anonymous crowd,
with hollowed-out eyes, are smudged in a fog.
Her heart a bird's, the net a snare.

An arc of triumph, forming, performing,
the crowd, amoeba of admiration.
Focussing on her end-point, perfection,
achieving initiation and forgetting.

The dizzying flight, the familiar net,
where she had plunged from the heights, her first fall.
In the crowd, one stares, who once knew her soul,
as it dived downwards, that night black as jet.

The crowd, an array of eyes, amoeba of lives,
she catches his glance, she wobbles, she gasps.
He knew "her pilgrim soul", aeons ago.
She glances downwards, feels dizzy, she dives.
Then she finds new wings, with a swarm of wasps,
"a lonely impulse", she flies and is gone.

Bridge-builder

Floods submerge houses, bridges break.
Noah's ark is needed in England this week.
The water rises, panic reigns.
Boats and helicopters, rescue plans.

Big G. flies in,
to stop the rain, to show his face.
It's not his fault that the bridges broke.
He can only help.
Better than news of Bombs or War:
A Natural Disaster.

Shake a few hands, share a few hopes.
Say our senior citizens are special folk.
In forty days and forty more nights,
will their homes be warm, and water tight?

In forty days and forty nights,
cameras gone, nights very long.
Will the ark now rest on dry ground?
Will the covenant bind, once the rain has gone?

The Lottery of Forgotten Things

The Lottery, I could play for money,
or play just to stay alive.
And if I win a load of dosh
I'll put it all in a great big tin
to give to "Perfect Hens Appeal",
for hens with gold-tipped wings.

The Lottery, I could play for dosh,
or play to dodge the bombs.
A bomb blew up when I was young
in the postbox outside my door.
The IRA were knocking there.
Knock, Knock. Who stares?
Just a letter for you.

The Lottery, I could play for bottle;
a bottle of booze, letter from a friend.
Out of the blue, they return,
like boomerangs.
They keep coming, coming back.
Back to front in time, yet out of time.
Mirror images dazzling the mind
reversed, like lights in the rear.
Be careful how you steer!

The Lottery, I could play for Love.
That word, such promises,
rose gardens. Promises of primroses,
We rose one day in the Lottery Garden.
The close of that day was a rotten garland
around our necks. The worm of decay.

The Lottery, I could play to stay alive,
to stay sane, if sane I am,
to welcome back the wacky returns,
the dew once more, or frost at dawn,
the twists and turns, the sparkling
wings of forgotten things.
Be gentle as you touch the golden tips!

DNA Lottery Sonnet

Lovers in the heather on Lammermuir,
castles in the air above them turning.
Sharp blades are tilting, bracken burning.
These windmills are good, our lovers are sure.
A poor forked animal fucks in the sun.
Its DNA demands fornication.
Chromosomes cross and cause procreation.
The beast fast asleep, genes journey begun.
Sensitive, lunatic. Don Quijote.
Chromatids anchored at the centromere.
Lovers oblivious, only kisses.
Genes for us all, partitioned grotesquely.
Our dreams turn above, in the stratosphere.
Sharp the puzzle of our noughts and crosses.

Consequences

See the rabbits burrow, they run and run.
Tunnels, dark and dank, ramifications.
Further in. What's done cannot be undone.

To follow the string back and back is tough,
through the maze, the days, the complications.
Will the plot reach out, have we had enough?

Out out damn spot. Cut out, said the doctor.
Quack quack, said the duck, in fascination.
Good chemicals can target a tumour.

The sequence is set, it colours humour.
It's all in our genes, alienation.
Her jewels were fish's eyes, hair a flower.

Ophelia floats, a picture, face up.
Great aunt drowned, I say in agitation.
Roots in a pond, queen of hearts, or ace up.

Voices

Two strangers across a table, a surreal interview.

Tense and judgmental, a life dissected, in loud voices.
I was right to be proud, my assailant stressed,
proud of my husband, proud of my career,
proud of having sacrificed him, to my dominant desire.

And she smiles at me, satisfied, as I crumple in a pile
of torn up CVs and decrees
absolute.

As I leave, the voices tell me
quietly: "It's time to go."

Hovering on the Edge

Fantasy zooms. Theosophy looms.
Thoughtful ghosts hover in tombs.
The living exist to harbour the dead.
The lead weight of ancestry, its breast on my head.

They hijack my thoughts. They talk and they talk.
Ideas like plastic, meaning not plus not.
Reality mixes, the colours all run.
What I thought was purple, is prose and onion.

A rose is a thorn and a thorn is a rose.
Sweet talking will prick you, or trick you with love.
The square is circled, the circle is queered.
Not wired for the light, I find it quite weird.
A strange bunch of roses. Theosophy flowers.
A coven of witches - I hover and cower.

Stitch-up

Like a needle it aims for the heart,
with an archer's art, sharpened past need,
a done lover ditched.

Self the only measure, the ego, the "I need",
result, cruelty. How cleverly it aims
at past needs, an eternal schizophrenia,
benefit culture party bonanza,
that claims, that blames us.

I reel as I stitch up the pieces of my heart
from the scattered tatters, discarded in the ditch,
worn and torn with wear, like the done lover,
threadbare.

Noose of Wire

Impaled in Dante's Purgatory, their eyes still haunt me.
Their thoughts were blind, sewn up with iron.

Their eyes were sealed, old lies revealed.
They lean together, whate'er the weather.

Coveting another, another was torn.
Clothes in shreds, bare flesh forlorn.

A tear was shed, departed shade.
A night flight turned to fear instead.

Excuses lame, penitential shame.
Each sealed vision its soul did claim.

Their string of eyes had spied the prize.
A hawk was tamed, its vision tied.

The talk is lame, the walk is snared, the prize
despised is justified. The love denied, crucified.

Disunited they wander, wound on an envious spool.
United and wounded, on a "thread of wire", so cruel.

Chances

A Bleak House, the moan of the wind.
Yellow snow of kith and kin.

A deadlocked home, a child alone.
Uncharted hurts are chanced upon.

The Chancery Court, a heart of stone.
Gross corruption, mind of iron.

Jaundiced and jealous, bitter and hell-sent.
Yellow flies buzzing, in icterus house.

Oh bleak midwinter, the howl in the web
is equity's moan. Thy Will be done.

The Seven Selves

The seven selves shiver, a cracked mirror quivers.
I hide in the crevices, I crouch in the corners.
It jumps like prejudice. It judges, fudges, unlodges joy,
and lodges its claws with anger in my crevices.
A jaguar won't hesitate.

Stevenson wrote of the divided selves,
Borges the mirror, the symbols, the jaguar.
I write of blindness, not of eyes but of prejudice,
and the hurt of a claw that should touch us with tenderness.

With the number seven, where to begin?
The seven secrets, or the seven sins?
Mysterious sacraments, or the metals and the planets?
No, I will write of the rainbow, and the colours that it brings.
When red I am hot, when orange juicy, yellow afraid, and green naive,
blue I am melancholy, indigo pretty, and violet a flower.

So in the early morning, when the seven selves shiver,
and the cracked mirror quivers on the edge of the dawn,
I will choose my colours, my rainbow of humours,
and lose my primordial terrors.
I will welcome the jaguar, with all his horrors,
into my heart and into my home.

Shakespeare

This great globe of tears rolls down his face like a sphere.
Our Shakespeare! How he acts each part, each hero's art.
Macbeth's ambition vaults, while Hamlet hesitates.
Othello blind with jealousy, Juliette with love.
Kind Lear, a fond old man, demands love, and is cursed,
while Gloucester's open eyes are plucked.
Was that act rehearsed when the actor learned to lose
his self in a lonely soliloquy? You, me, mankind, we see
his stories in our own globe, yesterday, tomorrow and forever,
and we see them carved from a modern mortal coil,
that rolls from our eyes, like a great sphere
of eternal human tears.

King Lear in the Storm

by John Runciman

The roaring sea in my mind rolls as I once rocked.
The demon waters rise, my devil's flesh is broke.
The wild white horses gallop, and come from the far shore.
I am left behind in the crack, with the world's worst whore.
My thoughts have crashed, my wits have turned.
I am poor, infirm, and have much to learn.
The storm is pitiless, my own flesh worse.
As a wretch I feel the thunder's curse.
Oh Fool, please help me, to see as you see.
Oh Fool, speak truthfully, what shall be shall be.
Frost bites your body, wind blows your mind,
your eyes are icicles, your ears are unkind.
Oh Fool, advise me, help me survive.
You will die when the wheel turns, so let your mind fly.
You will lie when the waters rise, and white horses sigh.
You will rest when they toss their heads,
and fortune reads her final lines.
You will know when the play is done,
on this great stage of rogues and fools.

The Choice is Open

"Totality of life and death"
like Christ the Saviour on the wrack,
his human pain tight like a vice,
his mortal condition a sacrifice.

The halo he wore did not show
the depths of the love he bore.
Only the dark hole of the soul
could synthesize and make whole.

A story of man and God
or son and overpowering father?
A journey chosen, a narrative spoken?
Was the path taken imposed or given?

The fork in the road, the choice is open,
for the one not taken, are we ever forgiven?
The past is how we got here.
It is gone but we live it, so near.

With arms and legs spread on the warped tree of life,
do days of past glory comfort or guide?
Do days by a throne of "excelcis and gloria"
ease our distress or lessen our agony?

"This body hanging on the Christmas tree"
is Agape for you and me.
The wrack of vice is now a wreath,
His fate, his sacrifice, our Feast.

The Ones That Got Away

A faint glow, a glance in the eyes,
Hints of lost futures, all the "ifs" of my life,
The names blur, the details flicker.
They have faded now, the objects desired .

A snatched bag, address book lost.
A train leaving a station,
those eyes drawing mine,
as we each go in different directions.

Oh fantasy, imagination.
What was real, what was delusion?
Fabrication, hallucination, a fig-leaf,
Figment of temptation?

My life and candles, from chance and choices,
for the lives of others, those other objects.
The fire flares then ebbs, the embers remain.
A faint glow, a glance behind.

Years

I was eighteen,
You were late.

I was nineteen,
You were mine.

I was twenty,
You were empty.

I was twenty one,
You were gone.

I was yours,
Too many years.

SkateRaw

We skated at Balgone.
The ice on the lake has long gone.
At Skateraw we water-skied.
We were raw, in those days of yore,
innocent to the core.
No threat of death spoiled the thrill,
of youth eternal.

Now Torness reacts,
it splits and cracks the atoms,
where we cycle.
We circle the station,
men fishing, the sea sparkling,
on our left.

Close by I left a gallery space,
a flitting crowd, to gaze at a young face,
in an old photo.
Demarco spoke of art, and remarkable times.
I sipped my wine, as I posed too.

There at Skateraw,
a raw fresh face looked out from a wall.
Love conquers all, I once thought,
like fission, splitting.

My lost husband was part of the wall,
encapsulated, trapped,
an artefact,
a butterfly that is dead and cannot fly.
Like an insect trapped in eternal youth,
he never cracked,
he never left.

Ideas fly free, and art,
in this space, in this place,
where we skied the waves,
in that innocence of yore.
I could skate on water,
or flit like a Painted lady
on a buddleia,
long before
a nucleus cracked,
Torness to the core.

Gathering-in

Gathering the fragments of my dreams,
these figments I clasp to me.
Close, and clear I see
how they rise, aspire
through the crisp autumn air,
how they soar
past October's spire,
where the church bells wail,
and the tomb stones are numb
in the deadening dawn.

Gathering the apples in,
the autumn sun sits
red around a silver rim.
Whispering our song again,
a lilting tune, sweet afternoon,
where laughter roamed.

"Gather your rosebuds while ye may" -
Herrick advises "marry".
Arise, aspire, as paths collide
to grasp the fragments, merry.
At first, too soon, the sun arose
and then we knew a sweltering noon.
Rise higher, and higher,
past dreams and the steeple.
A thistle, a rose,
a thorn or a petal.

Union Bells

On the castle hill above the Cam
stands the motte of the man
known as William the Conquerer.
Close by, some marriage vows were sworn,
for better or worse, to ride the storms.
One day in nineteen eighty one,
there were no bells, but there was fun,
the man Anglican the woman Presbyterian,
a happy wedding, a widening vision.

From the summit of the motte can be seen,
New Hall, its dome, a future's dream,
St. Luke's, its spire, a settled scene,
and famous colleges, like Kings.

Listen carefully, for a bell rings,
St. Giles, close by, is chiming,
a christening is coming.
The child is wearing a long, long robe,
an ancestral gown, that is Presbyterian.
The Anglican priest kneels down.
He touches the water,
the candles flicker and flutter.
The father does not falter
as he voices his vows.
The quiet mother watches
the candles with horror,
afraid that the white gown
could suddenly burn,
in an unholy union,
consumed,
like a vow that is broken.

Once, in another St. Giles
the bells rang out,
for a famous Union of nations.
The tune for every Edinburgh ear,
"Why should I be so sad on my wedding day?"
rang out, in fear.

Kata Beach

A turquoise sea, with rows of fishing boats.
Crab Island, in the distance, children play.
The tourists sun themselves in rows. The day
is glorious. On salty waves all floats.

Behind hotels the tuk tuks zoom along
the busy street, no space for walking slow.
I jump away, as scooters, kids on board,
whizz past, and commerce shows its hundred smiles.

I'm floating in a haze of Asian sun.
The chanting of the Buddhist monks remains
and lingers softly round the beach
where weddings on the sand show hope. No guests
but photos, yes! And monks in orange robes
who bring eternal blessings, as time flows.

Away

Tomorrow Tomorrow,
No Sorrow, he said.
Yesterday Yesterday,
Yes, she said.
But Better days lie ahead.

We will go where lovers go,
where doves coo,
where rainbows grow.

This, your ring is sapphire and gold,
With this rainbow I you hold.
And he held her close,
but the ring was cold
and it hurt her nose
when he pulled
away.

I Met My Hero

Every night I met him, secretly, clandestinely.
Lady Midnight, he called me, his voice hoarse with mystery.

He stroked me with his velvet tongue, so soft, so gentle, then so strong.
It sucked me in, like destiny. His words were jewels in the dung.

He sang a song of Joan of Arc, her solitude beneath the smoke.
Such cruel flames; her broken heart was turned to ashes when he spoke.

Every night I met him, secretly, clandestinely.
Every night he urged me on, to be free. Just be free!

Like a drunk in a midnight choir, I sang.
Like a beast in an empty byre, I cried.
As a woman with lines on her face, I aged.
But still I met him, at Midnight, each and every night,
my hero, my sage: Cohen, sweet Leonard.
Singing, half drowning in the bath.

Honey

Your hips were thin,
Let us begin.
Your legs were long,
And strong, so strong.

You promised sweet,
A swing of song.
Your kisses on wings,
A lush hush begins.

Stripping and sinning,
Winning and stinging.
Wild as a wasp,
Was the end of the game.

Your sting has long gone,
Let us move on.
Like a bee in the rose,
Buzz buzz, so it goes.

The Key

I want to win
The key to your kingdom.
I want to waken the flame
Where you burn.
I want to turn your lock,
To open and rock.

I want to win
The key to your window,
To see the cocks stride
As they strut outside.
If I crow at dawn
I will cry at night,
'Cause I want your vision,
Your heart and your kingdom.

I want to win
The key to your vision,
To hear your whispering,
Music of the spheres.
Petals and scent
On the bed by your head,
A basket of sweet flowers,
Unfolds, like the hours.
This is the key to all wisdom,
Yours, mine, ours.

Elvis - Do You Miss Me?

Elvis - those hips.
Otherwise known as Sex.

Do you miss me tonight?
Deep in your dark grave
where one day we all go.

So, sex and death, as they say,
are things that make us free,
essential things, that stay
in the subconscious.

Do you miss me tonight?
You. Who? Which you?
The slim, trim Elvis of screams,
lure of love on your lips,
dreams of six beats, a fantasy
of the heart, from your hips.

Then you flip, like the wind,
changed, forever changed,
leaving bereft the girls left behind;
on the shelf, shaking,
blowing in the wind, the self quaking
with fantasy, with fate.

Elvis, those hips, those eyes, that voice,
your sonorous, delicious, poisonous vice.
Otherwise known as Sex.

A Valentine Clock

At sixteen two love birds cooing,
at seventeen what blissful wooing!

At twenty six it's the mating game,
twenty seven, a white wedding.

At thirty six a breeding ground,
thirty seven, toddlers abound.

At forty six they're divorcing,
forty seven, hormones jumping.

At fifty six a new beginning,
fifty seven, biology resettling.

At sixty six they're on two sticks,
sixty seven, it's bus-pass heaven.

At seventy six knitting and bridge,
seventy seven, the wills are made.

At eighty six the cooing begins,
and then the clock comes round again.

Dates will not wait, oh friend of mine.
So be my Eternal Valentine!

Invincible Summer

We were sixteen, that July.
We were invincible.
The boat rocked on the river,
the shimmer of light was immortal.
His biceps shone in the evening sun,
back muscles rippled like water.

I wonder now, was he
(as were Rushdie, Obama, and Yentob)
bowled over by Roth as he filled the bowl?
Was "Portnoy's Complaint" his own private play,
was a "Human Stain" also the product of his dreams?
While my imaginings were quiet, invisible,
stirring like the shimmer of the river,
the only discharge a periodical leakage of red haemoglobin,
which cursed me into silence
and took my breath away.

We were sixteen that September.
Our only spoken complaint - the summer ending.

A Deep Deep Hole

You were digging a hole,
from when you were young,
so as not to see
the people around you.

One day you fell down the hole.
I thought that might wake you.
I was wrong.

Taboo

Politics is taboo, and death.
What you do, your work, is taboo.
We don't believe you.
Opinions are taboo, just smile.
Talk about the weather or the food.
And for goodness sake, of all things,
no poetry, please!

Vigilant

Two ex-lovers greet me, then look away.
Their wives nearby watch carefully.

Correspondence

The letter fell out. Long and thick, the strokes
were known, familiar. And ink was red,
like raspberry jam, her favourite. The pen
a fountain. Nineteen eighty two the date.

So long ago. It seems so recent. Days
when they were close enough to hang around
together; not a thought for time, the wasp
that buzzes round the fruit of all our toil.

A box of junk, with rubbish from her life,
which still survives against the odds; a horde
of arbitrary things, of stuff for mice
to feed on if the cheese is short one year.

Her shed was full of vermin, so
her wedding dress was chewed and shitted on.
But yet this other box survived intact.
The letters fell out. Not a wasp in sight.

Consigned to the Museum

A model, made to change in the public area.
Young, alive, but an object none the less.
Her prepubescent breasts, nubile.
Aged fourteen she was something new.
Aged eighteen, past her sell-by.
Consigned to the museum
of archived fashion shoots
preserved in glossy magazines.
No paper round for that young girl,
her zero hours contract worth millions.
Did she blow it on a first boy-friend
or sink into shares
that could deal her more cards
of a life-time.

Amy, no cat-walk model
but jazz genius mad
with love and drugs
and back to black
in the end for ever.
Consigned to our screens
her perfect screams
of raw youth
captured and hung out
like she was hung up
by all who loved or hated her.
Not just music in a museum
but real raw life
blood-red like steak.

Decades and Seas Away

A paraffin stove, and books to the ceiling,
it's two in the morning, I'm still up reading.
Eliot, Joyce, Vallejo, Neruda;
the Wasteland, Dublin, the death of the mother.

The room next door has another sleeping,
exhausted from beer, philosophy, talking.
A wall between us, but always dreams;
we're now both seas and decades away.

Orphans are speaking through starlit Heavens,
a new form of radar, pulses through air.
That room is the navel, the scarlet centre;
where pens were born, spurting blood from veins.

Messages pass through ether and rainbows,
emails mix memories, whispering news.
Friends from a network of Heaven's connections
fill gaps in old stories, still to be told.

It's two in the morning. I'm still up writing;
thinking about that old paraffin stove.

Twin Rivers

The river Tyne, the river Tajo,
twin rivers, my twenties.
From dark Northumbria to bright Castille,
from "hinnie" to "chica sola".

Through Jesmond Dene we wandered free.
In Heaton we fell head, and deep, in love.
The Navel of the Peninsula was Hell on Earth
for orphans at large on Spanish turf.

Each river bred its own idea.
The Tyne whispering "I think so I am."
The Tajo rather, looping the loop,
galloping us down a path with no end.

The river is endless, the sage will say.
It's constantly changing, always alive.
We never swim twice in the same water.
It's best first time to capture the other.

We capture nothing "hinnie" replies.
The river is tasted, its drops expire.
The loops of the Tajo will join with the Tyne,
before my old love again is mine.

The Metro to Manors

Deep under the city I travel.
Firstly I go to Monument,
then change for Manors.
I exit the metro station.
All is new, all except
one brick building, alone, bereft, old,
one sign only that a past existed here.

I was once young here,
and the men whistled as I passed,
as I walked up the hill towards
the Polytechnic.
The men whistled as they stood up,
a short break from the building-site,
to watch the sight of a young woman
striding past.
En route to the Poly, or the Hospital,
The General, the RVI;
to put on that nursing uniform,
and bathe the old miners, who laughed with me,
"Hey Hinnie";
or to change bedpans or soiled sheets.

Today when the Metro stops at Manors,
I exit to a new universe.
Northumbria University beckons,
its sharp steel and concrete
say "look at me, at my design,
my silhouette so sharp against the skyline".

Layer upon layer of my old life
lies in this city;
above, near the sky, visible;
and below, against the earth,
mining the centre.
Memories etched in my brain
like a palimpsest.

Closer

Remember Morden Tower, where the poets read,
where Basil Bunting went, with "Briggflatts", stone on stone.
Remember, I do. I who young was taken there.
This tower, rounded, stones of an old castle wall;
this city Newcastle, with ancient turrets high.
New Chinese Arch, exotic, colour, lions too,
romance, Shanghai. The city celebrates the East,
and Chinese restaurants feed Geordies, tourists, all.
In Kuala Lumpur I saw Petronas Twin Towers,
in Penang Island snakes attract the tourist crowds.
I, being old, visited the Snake Temple there.
A Buddhist monk from China set it up. Live snakes
parade for tourists; they who should not hurt the beasts.
Near Morden Tower and China Town, by Gallowgate,
the University is housed, and ancient medicine taught,
the new things too, the biotech etcetera.
And overseas they teach the students, Singapore
technology, it's true; Malaysia, a School
of Western Medicine, a very good one too.
And not for snake bites only, no, for all of this
and that.
                                        And that is nearly all for now, from one
who went to Morden Tower to hear the poetry,
when she was young, romance in the stones. No medicine
for broken hopes, but words go on, from year to year.
The city changes. World is closer than before.

The Beach is Closed

Oh Hawaiian Holiday, how I longed for you.
Ten days in which to force Romance. Beginning, Middle, no sad End.
A story from the LikeLike Highway. Honolulu is not Rome.

Oh America, on entering you, you record me, interrogate me.
Aggressively. My fingers leave my mark.
San Francisco, Gateway of a Golden Age, your dream failed.

The surfers move, the ocean swells, Waikiki is home to all the Angels.
Aloha and Mahalo with no sad end, for a Hawaiian Holiday.

Then the malls meet the downtown, and the tone alters.
Money talks, talks of money. Cars and parking lots. Drives not walks.
The March skies open, rain drops like pearls. The sewage spills, a tornado kills,
Landslides knock houses from hills. "Desperdicios, desperdicios!"

I met a man on the Diamond Head, expert in the martial arts.
He could maim a man by a soft touch on the tender anatomical parts.
Off Pearl Harbour in a steel cage, where chemical juices mixed with waves,
in the filth and the sewage he dived with sharks, in spite of suffering a weak heart.

A fucked beach, a burst canal, dirt dumped fresh, cannibal fish flesh.
Oh Waikiki, fallen ideal. Detritus of a holiday dream, dumped like an April fool.
Somewhere between New York and Pearl Harbour
your rough hand invades the thread of my dream,
as you write, and the folds of my flesh, so I write.

Your heart so white as not to speak of diamonds or roses or pearls.
Your swollen pride enters the folds and hollows of my heart.
Presbyterian not Polynesian, but I can see.
American Imperialism does not fool me.
Falsehood, fallacy, flattery, I see and say:
Your fond funny fool has indexed an ideal.

On the LikeLike Highway I leave.
You're leaving me. I'm leaving you.
Left to right, I write.
Romance is Dead, The Author Lives.

Oh America, on entering me, you violate me.
On parting you have not changed.
I leave a parting gift.
Again, the folds and hollows of my index.
Left and right.

Leaving Burma

A bright red sun is rising on the river.
A fishing boat rocking; our cruise ship passes.
An open sea ahead, the sun now yellow.
We're leaving Burma; it's golden pagodas.

And smiles of children; flowers for the Buddha.
The Island Pagoda; our feet are all bare.
The welcome is equal; our boats are better.
My fat dollar notes; a boy's hopeless stare.

The estuary ahead; Malaysia beckons.
Little boats line up on the far horizon.
In Yangon market I bought jade not rubies.
The heat like a sauna; our ship cool, like home.
We walked through a village of bamboo houses.
An elephant once was shot near here - under this same hot stifling sun.

My Elephants

My elephants line up one by one.
Their trunks are too short, their tails are too long.
Some have ears that flap in the wind,
some have nostrils that twitch and turn.

My favourite elephant has a hairy chin.
He's sharp as a kite, and loves to learn.
But the public don't like him.
They say he's a fake.
He lay down straight and stroked his jaw.
So they lined him up to be shot at dawn.

The strongest bull was tops with the crowd.
He lifted tree trunks, was working hard.
Country gossip gave him the crown.
The circus cheered him on and on.

My elephants line up one by one.
Some have been shot, some carry on.

Ash Island

Lanzarote, white and blue,
green and black, volcanoes, dew.
Lacking water, ash collects,
for vines and oranges, potatoes too.

Central earth had risen high,
magma flowed like honey.
Millennia ascended here,
barbecue of flesh on fire.

Now it still can cook your meat,
mere centuries are buried deep.
Sir Walter Raleigh, poet, pirate;
hamlets perish, and words for war.

Cesar Manrique, his house, museum.
Volcanic bubbles, nature's rooms.
Art as salvation, magma, foundation.
Hot-tempered and fierce.

Prickly Lanzarote!

Cynthia

You call me Cynthia,
the moon, who alters
monthly.
I call you Walter,
the ocean whose waters
are empty.

You called me Queen.
My crown shone and ruled
like the moon.
I called you lover.
My virgin heart throbbed
with your voice.

Elizabeth I am,
or "Cynthia
the Ladie of the Sea".
Sir Walter Raleigh,
you have dared
to dupe and deceive me.

I am like the moon, a woman.
And you, as a man,
did me wrong.
Let "The Ocean,
to Cynthia" call,
heart to heart, forlorn.

A mere wronged woman I may be
but I have it in my power
to keep you long in the tower.
Or if I so decree,
for your virile virtues,
I may pardon thee.

Letters From Birth

We were born entwined, one heart two minds.
Severed at birth, to live on this earth, a miracle of surgery.
Our limbs were free to roam, on separate roads
and sit by separate hearths.

Sometimes we would meet in a crowded room
and recognize our twin through invisible glass.
We could watch our other half, but not touch.
We were split. Voyeurs applauded
such Siamese success.

We were still entwined, both hearts, both minds.
Joined by invisible string.
Like elastic it would spring from time to time.
The further we spun out, the closer we sprung in.
Ethereal, Like Ariel.

From Dundee to Dunbar, Dunbar to Dundee,
we wove our poetry. Invisible words, letters,
sent through darkened glass, a mosaic of separation.
Selves known through pain.
Conflicting claims, separate clans,
Seen through the pane of Eden.

From the rim of the moon to the dark side at noon.
From the yin to the ither, from the yang to the loon.
Moon huntress hunted, chaste Cynthia chased.
Meek but not mild, wild wolf lies with lamb.
From warm womb to ice-cold tomb
we seek our celestial twin.

We are still entwined, one heart one mind.
A miracle of surgery, to live in the world
with eight limbs so defined. The secret is invisibility.
We two are spirits, in our journeys, on our roads,
And only sometimes does soul clap, and we descend.
Then like elastic we spring again, so close together.
Our Siamese limbs fuse to one,
and we return unto the womb.

Love - The Word

The weight it bears, this little word of might.
Agape, Philia, or Valentine day rose.
It promises the world, delivers loads
of pain with pleasure; pricks us, sharp its bite.

The snake in Eden started all the Sin,
a garden innocent and pure with virgin Eve
and Adam naked, like the fruit and leaves.
The Serpent bit him hard; its venom in.

Agape should be best, a Christian love,
a feast of wine for all the world and God.
Philanthropy, Philosophy, a dove
of peace, endearment; all are good. It's odd
how still, we crave the scent of roses red,
the taste of apples, bitten maidenhead.

Whittingehame

A tiny church, a yew tree, famous grave.
An ancient tower, old man alone; the wind
the only voice still heard. Then larks will sing,
and hymns will echo down the nave.

And lupins in the garden, summer drinks.
My name has changed, I am a girl again;
my maidenhead intact. A manse like home was then;
the flowers still painting in perennial inks.

Oh Whittingehame, what names your walls have seen.
Affairs of state were born around these graves
and great men kneeled to pray; their breath like waves,
on oceans. Names now merge, those who have been.
And we who live enjoy the song of larks,
midsummer blessing, while a lone dog barks.

Whitekirk

I stand so high, I read in loud clear voice,
King David spied Bathsheba bathing near.
He thought her beautiful, he wanted her,
and summoned her to lie with him, no choice.

He then dispatched her husband back to war
to get him killed and punish him through spite.
So David, who could scale Goliath's great height,
now King, had shrunk in stature, sinister.

In this same church I was a child at prayer.
At Sunday School the Bible Stories spoke
of baby Jesus crying, Samson's hair,
and mother Mary, when the babe awoke.
The Holy Ghost had come and been received;
a virgin still, so Mary thus conceived.

Return Journey

Over the hedges, a wide view.
Whitekirk through Tyninghame,
East Linton, Dunbar.
As the little bus winded to and fro,
a different view of the edge of the hill.

The women chatter as they gather, for a getaway shop.
Pensions and bus passes, happy people at each stop.
We glide through the countryside, known but not known.
What once was country is now town.

Then the return comes, the corners' change.
Once there was a hall, where people met, one and all.
A field now empty, takes its place.
More food for farmers to plant and gather.
Trees by the edge, while the hedges grow.

A pretty village with big new houses. Quiet and tranquil.
But where are the voices that sang here before?
Deep under the earth by the church on the hill.

St. Baldred's Arch

Tyninghame Kirk on the bank of the Tyne.
The arc of a river, the shape of a spine.
Stones like bones, skeleton shrine.
St. Baldred's Kirk, the Glory Thine.

Saint Baldred

In multi-coloured glass, our Saint of Bass,
with shepherd's crook in hand, and pilgrims near;
his purple robes, I see, green waves I hear.
In Prestonkirk, a window, Heaven's Cross.

By River Tyne an ancient chapel lies,
a skeleton of faith at Tyninghame;
remains of cliff-top worship, at Auldhame.
Three parishes are linked by Baldred ties.

His hermitage on Bass Rock, wind a knife;
St. Baldred's Well, healing, when the sun shone.
To minister to each and every kirk,
he's three in one, a trinity of life.
In death he multiplies, his body gone:
our multitasking Saint is thrice at work.

North Berwick Breezes

The sun, the rain, September's wind and shine,
and lobsters on the pier, an outdoor meal.
It's continental almost, don't you feel?
The gourmets come from far and wide to dine.
Upon the lawn a plastic whale's jaw-bone
is pointing out to sea, to Fidra, Bass.
A replica of one worn out at last,
the crumbling antique, dust to dust, alone.
Upon the pier the lobster claws are chucked,
the tourist season comes towards its end.
The Sula sails on, Bass Rock and the Craig.
Winter is coming, get the gannets plucked.
The pilgrims by the Auld Kirk fall down, bend
their knees, those wanderers, their search so vague.

Berwick Law

The Law looks out to sea. And in its jaw
a giant crab is caught. That could be me.

The whale has lost its jawbone. Jonah swam
away, and took its teeth, to wear alone

at sea. His necklace circled round the Bass
and he became a crab, with magic claws.

His pincers sit upon the Law. They nip
sometimes. But not as much as you or me.

Pilgrimages

I come from Whitekirk on the hill, where there is a holy well,
well known by the pilgrims of old. There I was a babe in a long white robe.

I came to Fife on the Queen's Ferry, where the white cross and the sword
of heresy drew pilgrims of conscience. I was a child, and innocent.

In St. Andrews I walked with my pilgrim friend in thought, by the sea
and the soaring cliffs. We were young; only I live still.

I went to Santiago, a field of shining stars, where today's pilgrims gaze.
I lived in a world of words, of poetry, like a maze.

I returned to the tall tower, and the university beside the sea,
where student pilgrims walk the pier. There, by the East Sands, I was a mother.

I revisited that harbour, where imagination tracked a mid-life pilgrimage,
a muddled map. Scallop shells to these dear sands.

I went to Stanza, on a private pilgrimage, from Whitekirk my little village,
to follow old stars, my destiny, to cross the Forth, at Queensferry.
Of holy waters I have sipped, and words, not of heresy, but sweet of memory.

The Sun and the Shell

They came from the North,
past crumbling churches of Betanzos,
feet sore from the journey.

So many before, tired and crazed;
a bright yellow shell ahead,
its light in rays across the sky.

Two rivers become one,
a "Ria" of shellfish, deep on plate;
"pulpo", "calamares", "bacalao".

Pilgrims in all parts, paths join
the westward way to Santiago.
A star on high to guide.

Friends left behind, a different route,
hospitals and graveyards along the way.
Deep into the night they cried.

"Via crucis", stations of the cross.
Abandoned chapels, crumbling monasteries.
The way of sorrows in fourteen stages.

Churches, hermitages, bridges, rivers;
a boat on a mountain side;
stones by a bare cross, where someone died.

Memories of moments shared,
generations piled, layer on layer.
Communion of Saints; Day of the Dead;

They enter Santiago de Compostela.
Stained glass, stained lives;
and the sharp taste of "vino tinto".

Today a medieval spectacle;
cathedral crammed with cameras and videos;
back-packs from round the world.

Bishops' mitres; a saint's head held high.
Tourists become pilgrims; they kneel
among the vast stone skeletons.

A solitary nun, her voice soaring;
the stone space filled with song.
The vast vaults reverberate.

Celts gather, with Gaelic kilts;
bagpipes echo Galician "gaitas".
They gather in Santiago.

A bright yellow sun marks the Way.

Whitekirk Chorus

Sing high, sing low, sing Halleluja-ah!
For beauty of the earth, and sea, arise,
and let us praise now. Autumn leaves, red skies
at night, on Whitekirk hill, delight us all.

Another hill, a green one far away,
the rugged cross; the King of love, shepherd
to all, our guide and light. How great Thou art!
Sing hymns, rejoice, worship 'til break of day.

The silence of eternity will dawn
and peace float down from high as love divine.
Be still, our souls, begin the song of praise:
this vale of tears is neither yours nor mine.
Our eyes have seen the glory, like the moon
around the Bass, or morning on the wave.

Tracing Your Presence

A vase of flowers on my kitchen table.
Their lines trace your presence. You were here.

The silence of your absence, long, like the years.
But I hear you in my heart's ear.
Beating, throbbing, alive in the ever,
ebbing and flowing, toing and froing.
The waves lapping, the trains, coming and going.

A vase of flowers, a memory of meeting.
A moment to crystallize, to cradle,
like the babe I once held, and gave suck.
Their colour is cream, the colour of your hair.
You were here. Their lines transparent in time.
You are always here.

Tulips
(For Lucy)

Red and pink they glow,
in my Dunbar living room,
linking my home with you,
once here, no more in view.

Orange and red you glowed
and my heart beat rose,
as you stepped from the Berwick train.
In awe I gazed, half amazed.

You're all glamour and glory,
golden hair and London clothes,
clutching a bunch of bright tulips.
I hug you and hold you close.

Too soon you are gone again,
my border belle, my darling girl,
back to England where you belong,
past Berwick on the border.

So I'm left here in Scotland,
alone, where I longed to be,
in awe of a vase of pink tulips
and the strange tricks of destiny.

Salt-water Love

Lucy, daughter of light,
shine bright round the rim
of the world.

Lucy, from London to India,
fly light as the wing
of a bird.

From Dunbar to Goa,
the seas will waft salt
water love.

May the waves of the heart
of the world,
protect you and gently cradle you,
like a mother,
my daughter.

Where the Peewit Calls

In Vatersay Bay the waves lap.
Across the Atlantic my daughter lies.
I was out of range when she called.
The signal failed.

On the Barra bus I heard the news.
The signal rang through better and better.

On the Barra bus my heart-beat burst
in surges of song, a lark on the wing.

In Vatersay Bay the waves lap softly.
Near Horgabost, lapwing chicks flutter,
close by a chapel.

Across the world, New York, London.
Across the water, hold my hand.
Where the peewit calls, there I am.
Mother to daughter, Eternal Strand.

To Have and to Hold

I found a rose from the bride's posy.
I will keep it for ever.

I found her smile in a perfect photo.
Let her wear it for ever.

I found her dress in shimmering lace.
It will shine on for ever.

I found my child had become a bride.
Keep her safe for ever.

Eternal Strand

On Seacliff beach the waves lapped.
Across the beach my daughter splashed.
I was within reach if she called.
The Bass towered.

In Vatersay Bay the waves lap.
Across the Atlantic my daughter lies.
I was out of range when she called.
The signal failed.

In Brixton town a family forms.
Across the world, New York, London.
I am within reach, just stretch your hand.
Daughter to mother, Eternal Strand.

Incomers

A family of foxes roams the garden,
they feel at home, the cubs are playing.
They love the city, never knew the country,
this Brixton hideaway a perfect den.
At night they roam Atlantic Road,
Electric Avenue and Popes Road.
They scavenge bins on Coldharbour Lane,
eat chicken bones and Caribbean chips.
Reggae music fills their ears,
and ganja scent is high, Jamaica near.
Red tails mark their passing through the night,
while humankind, on parallel lives, sleeps
or dances, unaware of animal
activities. The local Urban Fox
then barks, his eyes light up, electric bright.
With loud and joyful music in his ears,
and Caribbean weed in nostrils,
he heads to his den, through Windrush Square.

Purring at the Moon

A garden in the city, birds; a cat
is growling at the moon; balloons are high
in trees, and birthday lights are twinkling; sky
is painted navy blue; stars are champagne sparks.

The apple tree becomes a dream; its juice
and sweetness, year on year, a gift from one
who once lived here, and now has gone, passed on;
its root and fruit a countryside set loose.

Its branches shelter animals and birds
and urban foxes raise their cubs near by;
the squirrels climb as high as high can be.
Sylvanian creatures, nursery to eternity.
Up high in tree, loud hoots, schoolmaster owl:
"Te woo". So Pussy cat purrs: "Miaow-ow"!

Starburst

To London,
                train a starburst.

Grandson in his cot.
A star in his new-found world.

Floating Not Drowning

A Granny floating past, her broomstick green,
she's young again, feels carefree, air her bed
and zest her fuel; gone the sense of dread,
as each grey morning woke, the morning walk to work.

She feels a teen again. She packs her case
so light, it's easy; can be carried, quite
the thing. No smart shoes, just a change,
and on her back a tiny rucksack. Yes!

A client rang to criticize her style.
"So sorry you don't like it, but my words
were learnt while young, they're mile ahead of yours,"
she said. "And now I'm unavailable."

She's floating upside down to London town,
her broomstick sturdy, clouds all bumpy bump;
her grandson in his hammock, smiling.
He knows she's got a special wish for him.

Lightening

Mother and father
become, like lightening
struck, parents.

A feather floating
reminds them of a past life.

Five Months Old

Your blue eyes huge in your small face,
they take in all.
                                        Little globes!

Leo

A beam of sunlight, like your hair, a spark
of energy, the future bundled up
in fun. You run and Granny chases you.
For now she can keep up - but not for long!

A voyage of discovery, a walk
to Herne Hill. See how cars are washed, and how
the zebra crossing is the place to safely
go. Or press the button, wait for green.

The cafe by the bridge is great for trains,
and watching buses pass, and pigeons fly,
because they live there, underneath the rails.
And dogs on leads go by. And all the world.

The sun is shining, golden like your smile.
In Brockwell Park the water fountain startles
you. It's wet, my goodness! What a shock.
The world is new. It's plural. Glorious!

This is the Photo ...

This is the one where you saw two helicopters land in Ruskin Park.
"Choppa choppas", you called them. And "nee-naws", ambulances to me.

Your look so serious as number two took off, the air in the park, whirring.
You almost forgot that Mummy and Daddy had gone to Berlin.

Mummy, beautiful in her bright red dress, Daddy in his special suit,
with blue, bidding farewell as they spoke of a wedding.

Your little eyes and ears taking it in so well, the tone
in Mummy's goodbye all you needed to know: They were going.

Now, as helicopter number two rises above your playground,
you are captivated, enthralled by this giant insect, whirring.

Just like the ones Granny has shown you on the flowers on the road by the park.
But bigger bees, much bigger. These are your very own "choppa choppas".

Running Between

Blond hair, blue eyes, the little boys are mad
about cars, and things that go. They run and jump,
and race ahead, a little look behind
to see if Mummy, Granny, saw their trick.

They grin, their jest for life is vast and bright.
It's natural to climb the highest tree.
The little monkeys want to swing across
the topmost branches, not a thought of fear.

Their blue eyes look ahead, the future lies
in all directions, just for them to choose.
A helicopter or a tractor goes
where it is told, through air, or plough through earth.
These boys I see, both running free,
but half a century runs between.

I Stepped Through the Door

The neon street-lights are on, though it is nine in the morning.
Granny says they are broken.
I will tell Daddy.
A train is approaching the bridge.
We run, Granny and me, to the tunnel to hear it thundering overhead.
The train is heading to London, to my house.
We are heading to Dunbar harbour,
to look at the boats.

At Lauderdale Park the little girl's cafe becomes my helicopter.
A race is being held on the lawn. I run and nearly win.
A dinosaur appears and the policeman (that's me) arrests it,
even though Granny says dinosaurs are extinct.
But giants exist.
Daddy is very tall so he is a giant.

The Rock Pool Beach is covered by crashing waves
and Granny says it isn't safe.
"And be careful of the cliffs."
The swimming pool has a giant yellow caterpillar,
with boys and girls flying out of its mouth.

At the harbour we can't see the seals.
But I like the nee-naw life-boat vehicle.
We cross a bridge that lifts up to let the big boats through.
In the Battery Island I play with the gravel with two little girls in party skirts.
We look at the boats in the Cromwell Harbour.
The big one must need the bridge to open up.

Granny says fish can live in the water,
but people can't, 'cause they drown.
But the rescue boats can save peoples, and divers are ok.
The big waves by the East Beach are scary,
and Granny says not to go too close.
The swing park climbing frame is hard.
"I'm hungry."

"I want to go back to your house, Granny".

Dunbar Cradle

Lammer Island, place of Isolation.
Fever was high, here they found haven,
sometimes to live, sometimes to die.
Little hospital, close by the sea,
somewhere between Lammermuir and Heaven.
Cradle them gently. Shelter them greatly.

Barometer rises, barometer falls. God
protect the shore and the ships, the fish and the oars.

See the Lammermuirs and the new moon
"Wi' the auld moon in her arm".
The herring hill to Lauder take.

Take time to mend the lobster creel, To fix a net
or save a wreck. On dry land let the storm break.

Let the words of the hymn, rise, and protect from harm.
Let us sing, from our haven:
"Oh hear us when we cry to Thee
For those in peril on the sea!".
Protect them greatly. Cradle them gently.

Fish for Financial Services

Sitting on my bench by the Bay, watching the tide roll away,
watching the children play, and the ships docked out on the sky-
line. Eating my chips with fish, wondering how long it can last.
Will our waters be swapped for pearls, to line wealthy socks and pockets,
leaving us gutted, strung up, salted like Dunbar herrings.
Only the grit remains. The oysters are all in Brussels,
Politicians feasting, passing the port, passporting,
trading our fish-rich waters for quote "equivalent" riches.
No shellfish for us, just shells, to string our children's bracelets,
while Shard-sharp sharks of finance exchange our lobsters for shares.
The Common Fisheries Policy will soon no more be communal.
We swim to an unknown shore. Gritty no doubt, but hopeful.
I wish a wish for the sea. Let it be Fish-Full!

Rush and Hush

The Thames flows softly, its estuary wide,
a vein of strength. The city beside
it, running, jumping, sleeping, dreaming.
The countryside beyond untouched.

Metropolis shopping lists of trivia,
and energy expended, nonsense.
The young ablaze, a race to win.
The country peaceful, play and swim.

Timing the Thames

A walk along the Thames, a walk through time.
Blackfriars, Tower Bridge, then further east,
where once I went when I was young.
Old docks in those days; rough and ready then.

But now they flock with tourists, cameras,
and selfie sticks, to show how we were here;
so close to towers of steel, the Shard, so sharp,
the Gherkin with its glinting lights.

The cranes lift cargo now, police patrol;
their boats with sirens, blue lights flashing, noise.
Young men with muscles bursting from their youth,
are suited, sharp, with tie and collar, smart.

And now the Globe is hosting groups of kids,
where once the bard did tread upon the boards.
And Simon Poet puts his Odyssey,
along with Hamlet, showing nowadays.

"To be or not to be." That is the quote.
To be here now, or better still in past
time. Memories are made of movement, like
the river where I once saw rough tough trade.

End of the Rainbow

Pot of gold, end of the rainbow,
dissolves in sunlight. Watch the view.
Children running, reaching out.

If they could get there, riches galore
across the golden corn-fields shouting.
It was there. But it was where?

Their future, brighter, so bright yellow.
Children running, golden hair.
Three girls, two boys, behind, and little.

Half a century rushes past.
Three girls eating from wooden bowls.
No golden tresses, their aging hair.

Two boys at last have found the pot,
gleaming and shining at father's bedside.
Full of a warm and golden liquid.

Map Trap

The child is father of the man. The moon
is woman's flesh. A cheese is cut to feed
the mouse. The trap is waiting, watch it bang.
Its tail is long and stiff, now dead. So still.

The man is father of the boy. The sun
is shouting, you're the best. Your flesh is strong.
It's oxen heavy, pulling every load
with ease. The trap is set. The boy falls in.

The moon is made of cheese with holes. Its arc
is cradling boy and man. The sky is wide.
The road ahead is mapped with stars, so clear
for all to see. But when the cheese is served
with bread, the constellations shake, the plough
falls down to earth, and maps are torn to shreds.

Down

I brushed your baby-soft down.
Little duckling who turned to a swan.
Your beak became skilled
at seeking out worms.
My wings took me away.
Upwards.

The Oak's Sails

Grand old man of the woods,
your leaves like sails in the wind;
your acorns, twins with wings,
float downwards to the ground,
where you belong.

Grand old man of the Druids,
your mistletoe sacred,
its white juice like semen,
its kiss a secret.
Fertility's omen.

Grand old man of the world,
your branches support,
birds, squirrels and beetles.
A carbon taker, an oxygen maker;
your wind is our future.

Grand old man of the seas,
your timber strong ships;
your beams tour the globe,
float the oceans, the world.
High wind powers your sails.

Twin Nativity

"It's a boy", cried the shepherd.
"We followed the star", cried Balthasar.
"It had to be a male child", cried Melchior.
The phallus foretold the birth.
The shooting star was seminal.

Ah, ah, ah, moaned Mary.
This manger is too small for two.
"For two?"
Joseph just about jumped from his gown.
"Make the oxen move over", she yelled.
"Move over, great beasts" ordered Gaspar the Wise.
"Let the lady lie there."

And there in warm damp straw
where the animals had lain,
was born a girl-child, called Jane.

Miracle in the Manger

A humble stable, animals, and faith.
With Joseph praying deep into the night,
as Mary suffered by his side, her breath
the pain of all the world, her fear the screams.

The baby born, a miracle of love.
Where nature broke apart, the Holy Dove
came down, and God became a man.
A woman's womb immortal, breaking blood.

The donkeys bray, the baby cries, the straw
is soft, and Mary floats away in clouds
of joy. Joseph kneels again and thanks
the Lord for this great act of Power, Might,
and Glory. Thanks be given now, on High.
In Heaven the bells sound. Donkeys kneel down.

An Angel Comes

The egg has cracked -
                    and the bird escaped.

Its beak is open. Milk, more milk
for me, it cries. Its scream
a tearing of the womb. Its tongue
cut, to latch more gently.

Mouth to nipple. Eve bit the apple.
Juice escaped from her lips
and ran down her legs
like amniotic fluid.

The baby is asleep. His face
reflects the angels.
His eyes are stars.
His breath is soft as feathers.

His birth came as a mirage -
                         a morphine miracle.

From the Stable to Eternity

Give thanks for the birth, red wine in the cup.
Forget the pain, give praise. For a life delivered.
Divine intervention. A baby unable to breath.
Give thanks to God, the invisible, capable of miracles,
for ten little fingers, perfect, and ten little toes,
pointing the paths to eternity. Give thanks for breath,
for air, for a little dear, whose entry to this vale of tears,
sucked his lungs, and pierced his heart, his nose, his arm.
Forget his battles for oxygen, with the oxen standing by,
their horns ready for any necessity.
Give thanks for the mother, alive still.
Nature, mother of all, gives all, takes all.
So kneel, humbled by terrible destiny.
Receive the Holy bread and the blood-red wine..
Sip from the cup. And give thanks again.
Thank God! Amen, Amen, Amen.

Halleluya, How He Loves You!

The baby cries, the manger rocks, and rolls
around. The cattle hum a Christmas tune,
and chew the cud. The three Kings kneel and pray,
their gifts are not OK for babies. The star
had dazzled them, befuddled them. The gold
they spent on whisky made them merry, but
the myrrh has scared the donkeys. Now
the camels bolt, and Joseph says:

"Enough's enough. My wife is tired. The baby cries.
The party's over. Please get out, you lot."

The Magi leave. The manger rocks. A tear
then drops from Mary's eye. At last, some Peace!

Chewing the Cud

What does Christmas mean for you or me?
A lost Eden around the fire, of an old dear family,
of chatting happily, with mother and father, all in the old order.
Of singing carols all in line, of candles and pine cones and hot mulled wine.
The advent calendar spoke of the time when baby Jesus was born like a lamb
to shine in our lives as a mere man, while through his veins his blue blood ran,
royal, immortal, like time's vast sands.
The manger with the mangy stock, the shepherds watch, star struck,
the cattle stand and chew the cud. Mary and Joseph could cuddle.
So pretty with its Christmas crib, the babe on the cards does not cry.
Let's sing for the mystery of the lost fire of Christmas.
Let's arise and pick up the fallen apple of Paradise.

Holy Cow!

Watch the night candles cradle the sky.
Watch the bright angels plough on high.
See the stars furrow, the stable below.
Know the royal city by the song and the glow.
Sing out loud our watch-night carols,
excelsis, glorias and hosannas.

You've shopped and flopped, bargained and queued.
You've rushed and stressed, and drunk like a newt.
Now you've earned your rest, 'cause holy Christmas
glitters at last. Now all can worship the fat golden calf.

So sing Hallelujah for peace on earth.
Let's say I love you, but not on my turf.
Good will unto man, Unto women as well.
Hells Bells! Let them ring.

Let us sing, sing, sing -
As shepherds watched their flocks of old,
Hosanna in the Highest!
The cattle in the stable became glitter and gold.
Holy Cow! Happy Christmas.

Latest News:
Jesus Christ Had a Twin Sister

Latest Views:
"Blasphemy", said the Preacher.
"Gender Wars", said the Feminist.
"Genetic manipulation", said the Scientist.
"Liable", said the Judge.

"A plain old fashioned lie", said the old lady.
"And what would become of the Marys?
Where would they be in the eternal story?
The Mother of God playing second fiddle.
And Mary Magdalene, well, hey diddle diddle !"

"More Blasphemy", said the Preacher.
As the cow jumped over the manger.

Still

A young girl running along the strand.
Her mother's billowing skirts beckoning.
The mounds of petticoats will hide the child
from prying eyes in the ice cream van.

A woman, young and beautiful, pursued
by virile suitors, beaus on bicycles,
who leap through hoops to please her mother too.
But they are snared, their necks are trapped, and snapped.

An old female, with creaking bones, and frail,
boils barley soup in a copper cauldron.
Still hanging round her mother's skirt
she feeds the Old Hag.
Then heads to the whisky still.

No More Porridge

Once upon a time - a glorious line.
This was the start - she said with a tear.
There was an old woman, who used to dine
on porridge, and cow's milk, and homemade beer.

The porridge was good for her - made her strong.
The milk was so sweet, she felt like a calf.
The beer made her dance, and hum along.
The gramophone played on - an hour and a half.

The cat was purring - it took her fiddle
and played a very melodious tune.
She wanted more milk - hey diddle diddle -
but the cow jumped over the moon.
The old woman rose, and looked through the window,
as her dish ran away with the spoon.

No more porridge for me, she said.
But then, I suppose I'll soon be dead.

The Black Sheep

Amy, Amy had a lamb,
its tail was black as soot.
They put it down the chimney pot,
it came out bruised, from head to foot.

The chimney, it was nicely cleaned,
the fire burned charcoal, logs, or beans.
The beans were baked in a frying pan,
potatoes toasted, with bread and ham.

And Amy, Amy's little lamb
was fried with eggs - so sad I am!
Its tail was black but its heart was gold,
this tale's old hat, but it had to be told.

A blackened sheep down the chimney pot,
the aroma of a good hot pot.
Now the victim is just hot air
and exhausted family table talk.

Gifts

My regiment of women gave me books to cook by.
With chicken wing stew I got by.

At Christmas I gave my teenage daughter Delia Smith
and Jamie Oliver. A new guilt gift each December.

My sister's recent recipe gift, "Under the Pot Lid". The Queen
and Ladies Curling Club, on opening the cover I discover.

Must be a joke I tell my daughter. When I can buy good pie
at the butcher, or banana bread with the organic vedge.

But it really was no laughing matter, I should have known
my batter better, and regulated my oven's temperature!

We are judged on our cakes, and on how they are baked.
At the last blast in my regiment, they will ask if my buns burnt!

The Matriarchs

How they arch their brows, our matriarchs.
So proud of their traditions. See how they position
us in their ark. So hard they work to mould and make us.
They scold and rate us, mediocre by standards superior.
So hard they worked at ironing, to keep their men earning.
Their world as wide as the county, the countryside, its breadth
the breath of privilege, its scope the sound of ting-a-ling.

Now get your houses clean, 'cause if you slack
the matriarch will frown and point out all you lack
in morals, purpose and all that!

Spreadsheet Puddings

Our Christmas pudding, round and plump, is ripe
for cutting. Candles burn around, and rum
is poured on top. We watch it burn, and wipe
the sweat from stressed-out brows. So bang the drum!

At last the spreadsheets put away, we sway, and eat.
Redundant puddings welcome now, their taste
their own, and special, whether sour or sweet.
Not even awkward meringues put to waste!

The familiar circle welcoming
the sherry trifles from a packet; tarts,
and chocolate cake. Please have another helping,
from sweet round puddings. Place your hands on hearts:
Next year, our Christmas puddings' rings of fire
will not circle Hell, or be kept on file!

The Angel's Wand

The Angel on my tree has a big knife.
Her smile is wide, her wings are glistening;
and fairy lights sparkle. She is the life
and soul of Christmas. Are you listening?

She waves her wand, and long thin streamers fly,
with useful instructions for a perfect pie.
She stomps her feet and snowflakes float about;
so close to Heaven she could sing, or shout.

The Angel's knife is sharp for cutting meat;
the turkey must be sliced the proper way.
The little Christmas decorations hide.
They meditate, and dream of joy and peace,
and all things simple, a special day;
for those of us who still on earth abide.

2016: An Ending

The year is nearly over. War and bombs
to close its final chapter, children dead,
and Christmas shoppers slain for festive fun.
So where on earth to now? Six feet below?

The year is nearly over. Trump and May
now hold the reins. And little ponies, dogs,
or other animals must trot and jump
to their new earthy tune: "six feet below".

The year is nearly over. Count our gains,
and losses too. We won the virtual world,
we lost the real EU. A mirage shone
and blinded us, its light aglow, then gone.

A new year clearly stirring, earth is strong.
The young are walking, talking. Listen now
and you will hear them laughing. Flashing lights
a mirage from on high. Oh Glory Be!

Resurrection

Autumn red and gold, rosehips shrivel.
Winter approaches, shivering and blue.
New Year, a dark Isle, on the far horizon.
Springtime roses burst into view.

Renewal

New Year came in with voiceless hugs.
The dancers bowed, no Strip the Willow. Dumb
or croaky, like a frog, whose throat was through
with talking. What are words for, we can rest!

The next in line was bright green Sputum.
It grew in new year lungs, like slime.
Awake next morning coughing loads;
the basin full of its creative growth.

The days went by in daze of TV, bed,
and when old voice returned, the telephone.
The fever peaked in sweat, and search for temp
machine. The digital thermometer
was missing, absent, like a mind, away
on higher planes. Like no to antibios,
like no, these lungs could work alone to oust
all aliens, to oust these Old Year omens.
Then Strip the Willow, up and down the line,
in time. Then step we gaily through the swamp.
We sing, amphibian friend and I.
We sing out high! We shout and jump.

An Awkward Script

My skull I fractured long ago. My eye
was nearly lost. "It popped", she said, as blood
was pouring down my face and on the car,
which upside down had seen its last. Smashed!

The scaphoid bone, it never heals. The hand
has far too many bones, the doctor said.
These little ones are lost. The dogs that knocked
me off my bike were only playing. Pain
remains, reminds me of the time I fell.

The stitches round my eye were neat, well done.
The night-time doctor, handsome, kind. He sewed
my face in layers, my eye was safe
behind the skin of scars. The fear
of cars remained. And now again, the pain
a dull ache, eye still seeing clear, but skull old.

My hand still holds a pen, my fingers clutch.
I write an awkward script.
I scribble down:
Scaphoid fracture healed.
Popped eye congealed.
Skull bone cracked.
Brain remains intact.

But upside down, I fear the last.
And inside out, I fear the blast.
I hunt for key, turn engine off.
The dogs still bark. I hit the ground.
The car has roof on road. My face
is sticky. Blood!
                    I wake. Alive!

Cutting to the Bone

Halleluja! A child is born.
Aged one, aged two, aged three, aged four.

Walking to Sefton Park we witnessed the attack.
A man beat up another man. A broken rib, a cracked hand?

Multiple rottweillers, no muzzles.
Mummy, Mummy! Running, running.

Pavements heaving. Shit on shoes.
Child brings it in. The filth, I mean.

Falling, falling. I was cycling as the dogs circled.
Bang - my cracked hand.

In Wavertree this week, a Pit Bull killed a child of four.
"Injured grandmother fought Pit Bull terrier."

Handle with Care

Handle your Joints with Care:
Stretch and Nourish, Swim and Balance.

Handle your Kindle with Care:
Read Physiotherapist, Bookmark with Discretion.

Or Crash Bang and Splinter:
Two hundred Books, one Bone, at a Canter.

Archived, their Titles:
Alphabetical List, Shell of Themselves.

Joints in Action:
Content Emptied, Cracked and Dry.

Find Essential Wifi:
Rejuvenate, Elasticise, Revitalize the Mobile Library.

Preserve those Ancient Habits:
A Book on every Journey, not Vulnerable to Accident.

Or Write on the Moving Train:
Massage the Sedentary Hours with Care.

Chronic Fog Syndrome (CFS)

The worm was cold; the woman warm.
In hibernation worm survives, suspended animation.
Woman lives, tired out, post-viral, ill.
Exhaustion rules her wintry kingdom. Chilled!

The worm has entered "dauer" state; a stasis.
Waiting, months on end, metabolites
all changed, their profile like the woman's blood.
Fatigue its meaning. Pain her syndrome.

Such harsh conditions hit the worm, it shut
its systems down and waited 'til the time
was right to waken, stress all gone. Such harsh
conditions hit the woman, she felt dead
as "dauer" locked her in its tower,
body bound in pain, and brain in chronic fog.

Bone Marrow Gifts

Stem cells, chemotherapy, cord blood. Irradiation, haemoglobin.
Bone Marrow Transplantation. How many lives are saved?

Lymphoma, leukaemia, thalassemia. Myeloma, or sickle cell anaemia.
How many survive? How many die? What harrowing treatments?
As mothers watch their children fight, with graph failure, or growth factors.

Host or donor? Sister, brother; a son's bone marrow for his father;
a sister's stem cells for her sibling. A gift of life, or fatal rejection?

Each record in the database, unique number, not a face. Each cell donation
has its place; significance statistical, meaning medical.

Marrow gifts from kith and kin; flesh and blood bear witness.
Marrow gifts from faceless tribes; unknown donors, anonymous lives.

The Gift Relationship : Blood Transfusion *

August 2018:
Blood Corpuscles for strength, I thought.
I could do with some more of them.
As the world fell down around me,
circling, crashing,
leaving me lost as to who I am.
Too old for this game of giving.
Certainly!
Another thing I'd like some more of
is youth's energy, strength
and the ability to stay upright.

February 1983:
I arrived home a week later,
my skin paper thin, my face white.
You should have had a transfusion,
said my midwife.
Even from the depths of exhaustion I knew
that the hospital chaos prevented that.
The consultant with his phone off the hook.
Caesareans done, but not in theatre.
That five hour wait in the delivery room:
Bleeding!
It did not kill me,
though my doctor father-in-law
said it should it should have.
"Still the main cause of maternal mortality" he said.
Nor did the general anaesthetic
and a hand up my insides
knock all the stuffing from me.
Nearly, but not quite.

Think of the difference
if I had had that blood transfusion.
Think!
I would have been up and about and sparky so soon.
Then a few years later dying of HIV, Hepatitis C
or living for decades, a wreck of my former self.

A butterfly's wings can move mountains.
So give thanks to the old serendipitous God:
Chaos !

* Inspired by reading "The Gift Relationship" by Richard M. Titmuss, when I was a student nurse in the 1970s in Newcastle

The Gift of Life

The Dunbar waves waft me in dreams.
Beside me my mother, her coat on my shoulder.

Barcelona's port, my daughter sits by me.
Shellfish and lobsters, a restaurant by the sea.

The waves on my desk, water words, my computer.
Taut texts of energy, our planet's future.

Kinetic, potential, pressure, the swell.
Salt water, sea waves, The current's pull.

Past and present, round and onwards.
The waves of the oceans pulse at my heart.

Rhythms of ancestry, crosscurrents of destiny.
Tick-tock of the coronary artery. Eternal gift from you to me.

Lost

I lost my voice after the last Bar B Q, before you left for France.
Too much talking I thought.

I lost my voice after the last night that you slept by my side.
Must be a virus, I thought.

I lost my voice. After five or six weeks I still couldn't speak.
Think now, speak later, I thought.

I lost my voice. Depression, isolation, despair and no expression.
I was alone, I thought.

I lost my voice. The doctor put a tube down my throat.
Just mucous, not a tumour.

Caused by loss, he thought.

Mind Maps

The imagination mirrored
in medical imagery.
Art and inner thoughts
in arteriography.
Hallucinations shown
as lucid visualizations.
A CAT scan scatters
carotid artery angles.
Speech becomes graphics.
Tomography's words
are spoken in silence.

Toxic

The sky is blue, the water turquoise bright,
idyllic, peaceful, dreamlike, far from harm,
where wildlife roam and children breath fresh light,
the air so free, and rustling trees, a charm.

Beware the future looming close at hand,
recycling all the waste the flag commands.
It's coming near, they'll dump it by the sea,
where emerald blue meets fish, all green.

Intoxicating air with particles
too small to see, more deadly thus.
Where foxes ate and robins red once sang,
the cobwebs crowd the pool, and dust
to dust returns, as poison fills all veins.
Dioxins in the wind where horses neigh,
and brothers fight with sisters down country lanes.

Memories of Order

Aldershot summer, memories of order.
Army, church, routine, relieved only by the conkers' crack.
Chestnuts on strings, puppets to childhood's touch. Boredom beaten.
What Crackerjack cousins, taught me this nut to crack!

Such shining specimens brought home in a box,
To show and strut, so bright and clear.
Conkers conquering, armies on strings.
In their coffin they rot, a slow, sad, splitting.

Shots sound over Afghanistan. Who are the Taliban?
Our church is attacked, in London's tube war.
Heroin streets become a nightmare.
Memories of order, A mirage.

London's Burning

Ladybird, ladybird,
fly away home.
A helicopter hums,
gangsta rappers beat drums.

Ladybird, ladybird,
fly away home.
Blackbirds are tweeting,
blackberries sweating.

Ladybird, ladybird,
fly away home.
The hooded owl is hooting,
"Get out before the shooting".

Ladybird, ladybird,
fly away home.
Your house is on fire
and your children are gone.

All except one,
and that's little Mark,
who is hiding his spots
under a Facebook Mask.

Weird Week

Tuesday to Tuesday.
First day to last day.
Life without pause.

New York sent steel text,
twenty thousand words of it.

Brief pause, Dunbar,
I hear a real writer.
Then wave power
from Barcelona.

Pause two to Edinburgh,
more words, from friends,
on canvas now.

Then waves and oceans,
wind and turbines.
Energy to drive
our weird modern world.

As the song sings,
what a wonderful thing.
From our first day
to our last day,
as I said to myself,
is this wonderful world.

The Devil and the Creepy Blue Sea

I hear the Siren call of my mobile.
The thump of text messages beckon.
A thousand spam emails block my inbox.
Facebook tags bring unwanted comments.
My answer-phone flashes urgently,
as I arrive home.

Somewhere between Scylla and Charybdis
I am stalked by Facebook.
Between the whirlpool of "Friends"
and the jaws of gossip,
the noise is deafening me,
and I wonder how to communicate.

I have been told:
Don't text me because I can't see well,
and it's complicated.
Don't ring 'cause I'm too busy,
so I can't speak.
Shall I write a letter, I wonder,
and test the mollusc method?

We are connected yet divided,
we reach so far, yet not at all.
With self promotion, the Siren's song,
I fear we are lured towards our doom.

If I made a Scotch broth, or a good pot of tea,
and suggested some conversation,
what would the reaction be?
Would that not be a waste of time,
says my friend, as distance divides us.

And also, said the Devil:
If your hands are so idle,
just call me, on my mobile!

Ghost in the Sewage Machine

A ranting raving idiot I am.
My mobile rings, I run, another hassler thinks
I'm free. I'm not because since I began
this job, I live in sewer machines. It stinks!

So does the Chancellor, he stole my dosh.
My pension down the chute with all the dross.
You're old enough to work some more, he said.
That's fine, OK, work fast. Bang, bang, you're dead!

A midnight vigil, ghostly in machines.
Pre-treatment works, and nuts and bolts. Water,
the gift of life, so pure, so fresh, in deep ravines.
Or tortured from our waste in treatment plants.
Machinery of the text that thinks, my mind.
This translation of mine is hard, but soft. It stinks!

Deadline Sonnet

The word-pool is empty and grey today.
Meaning is glimpsed through a clouded mindset.
Nouns crowding verbs, sound different in hindsight.
The syntax has twisted and turned away.

Keyboard my fingertips, screen eyes my own.
Type quicker, think faster, a deadline looms.
Swing that subjunctive, make it play my tunes.
But Spanish idioms still linger on.

My tooth has broken, I need a new crown.
So translate faster, convert words to pounds.
Catch adjectives; passive goes to active.
Each year my hair falls out, less is still brown.
Change florid foreign tone to English sounds.
Words tap faster, I am in them, captive.

The Snake Pit

I try to square the circle, snake bitch bites,
so mouth to tail, and hand to snout, I'm out
in cold New York, where bitches shout
"Just fix it, slave; work nights".

So nought point naught one dollars is at stake,
she haggles, tries to cut my word rate back.
Track changes on, she mirrors her own lack
of grace; lines cut through words, strike out, and break.

A virtual circle, oceans far apart,
our city girl is climbing sky-scrapers;
from high she sees just towers, no sky.

While I below sense clouds as art,
and words form circles, dancing, capers,
and snakes in grass are trod on hard, and die.

Statements

Redundant tears in haste are shed.
New York accruals. New words, new rules.
Accountancy, consolidation,
accuracy, the wealth of nations.
Mergers and takeovers, branches, subsidiaries.
Words to hide, worse to reveal.
A balance sheet, a statement,
redundant tears in haste
are shed.

A Place Frozen in Time

Tiananmen Square, its massacre frozen in a smuggled tape,
which escaped via Tokyo. The one sent to Kuala Lumpur perished,
as did the person on Kate Adie's right, then her left.
Her arm took the bullet, which scratched her as it passed.
So she ran, to tell the world, to show the world the students
who stood for real against the tanks. (No imaginary heroism here.)
That square in Peking in 1989, wiped clean off the slate.
That June Incident in Beijing, a euphemism.
Do not let the people see the young students dying.
Their own children dying.
But Kate Adie froze their wasted young lives in time.
She, whose crisp voice is timeless, was incoherent,
as she reached the hotel, covered in blood and clutching a tape,
of a vanishing moment frozen in time.
But the desperate BBC images told the world.
And the clear articulate voice of a lone brave woman.

Glinting Steel

The day before we were in Malaysia,
a galleon from Portugal on show.
Malacca to Singapore, an easy trip.
Our ship a world apart, a floating globe.

Horizon of concrete blocks, sky above.
The sea below us, mirror, glass, and sun.
Our ship approaches, slowly. Land ahoy!
The concrete blocks grow taller, reaching high.

A taxi rush across the city next
to Changi Airport, where a garden grows.
Then soon we rise through air and see again
the concrete blocks; they shrink below us now.

Surreal now, the city glinting steel.
A wooden galleon could sail these seas.

Geoengineering

We will remake the earth, no seven day job.
Let us shield the sun's rays, the engineer says.
Let there be light, said God.

We waste our energy, excess use not harmony.
We guzzle oxygen, aviation, ambition.
We muzzle opposition.

Let us seed the oceans with iron eating plankton.
They will eat excess rays from the sun's solar field.
They will sink to the seabed, satisfied and well fed,
with seaweed and crayfish, the ocean made a carbon dish.

We will seed the oceans.
No seven day job, said man to God.
There is too much light. Too much carbon and heat.
We are the engineers. We know this is right.

Then hubris spoke from out of the dark.
It just could be, said he:
Each bright, bright day will be followed by night.

Explosive

Tectonic Plates are sliding. Global scum
arises, morphed, now man-shaped. Monster thoughts
to power continents, their shifting shapes.
Alliances, amoebae, fluid mass.

America or Europe, all a mess.
A mass of lies which mix, don't match.
Upheaval, muddle, broken promises.
Old friends have turned, old lines zigzag.

Tectonic Plates, an expert lie, no doubt,
or so they say, the new post-truth police.
But still they shift, these dogged continents.
The centre cannot hold again, and not
the first time. Gravity is strong, but mass
is also energy. It can explode.

Black Velvet

They spin their silk so fine, and gossamer threads shine at dawn.

I tried to write of spiders, their long legs, black as soot,
their shy demeanour, lurking near, then on the run,
alone, and soulless, horrid, so

I tried to write, but I just couldn't win.
My pen rebelled, forces within me said: "No!".

They're foul, they're hairy, scary, and they creep along at night.
Some say, like all God's creatures, they have soul,
but I deny it. It is not so.

Black velvet bodies, rounded; full of flies, and fangs with poison.
Hate. Or just something they ate.

A Cold Snap

Crocodiles lie in wait in Birnam Wood. They lurk in unexpected places,
awaiting snow. Evolved to live in extreme climates. They aim to stay.

The Hags are hiding in their tree-houses, casting spells
to control the forest. They see the future, can alter the gene
pool. Crocodiles were cooked in a crooked flask.
CRISPR-Cas their latest trick, to edit out the rotten past.

The ladies wait in Stirling Castle. Crocodile skin bags glisten like ice,
smooth to the touch, a symbol of glory. Ladies parade in their silken gowns.

The logs are moving in Birnam Wood. Melting ice makes hard ground shift.
Ladies groan in their four poster beds. Hags screech like owls in starless night.

"Crocodile crocodile, come dine with me.
Your genes are the future, we'll have them for tea.
Our skin will grow smoother, our teeth long and white,
and our old weary legs will be logs on the fire.
We will burn oh so brightly in this dark starless night.
Make the earth move. Crocodile: Light up our nights!"

And up rose the reptiles from their century-long nap.
With the ice in their teeth they gave a Cold Snap!

It's a Knockout

Three blind mice, three blind mice.
See how they run, see how they run.
A scientist comes with a knock-out gene.
Their running is faster, their seeing has gone.
Three blind mice.

Three blind poets, three blind poets.
Hear how they rhyme, hear how they rhyme.
They were knocked on the head by a microphone.
Their verses are sharper, their rhythms are fine.
Three blind poets.

Three blind muses, three blind muses.
Watch how they move, watch how they move.
It amused them to capture the artist's heart,
to set it racing, to knock him about.
Three blind muses.

Three blind knives, three blind knives.
They came from the house of the farmer's wife.
The mice were all dead, the muses had run.
Only the poets could knock her out.
Three blind knives.

Three blind phrases, three blind phrases.
A snip in line beats a stitch in time.
These genes are mine, but theirs before.
Blind to where we go on now.
Three blind phrases.

Three blind graces, three blind graces.
A one in three, a three in one.
So DNA for mouse or man.
Woman is graceful; mouse lost his tail.
Three blind graces.

Three blind spiders, three blind spiders.
See how we spin, see how we spin.
A poet comes with a nursery rhyme.
The running is faster; the rhythm is harder.
"Knock knock knock".

Who's there? asks the clock.
Homer, Milton, Borges?
Tick tock, tick tock, tick tock.
He can't read his lines, so he knocks three times.
Three blind poets!

The Long Tale

Curious,
how a mouse escapes down a hole.
Curious,
how a hole can be like a window.
Curious,
how a window can open or close.
Curious ,
how closely we relate to a mouse.

Curious,
How a mouse has a long tail.
Curious,
how a tail can be long or short.
Curious,
The short strand Y means male.
Curious
how the male pursues the female.

Curious
the female strands are all X.
Curious,
how Xs mean kisses as well.
Curious,
how well the long tail draws chance.
Curious,
how chance has a science of graphs.

Curious,
how it flees off the edge of the graph,
the last to be seen its long tail.
Curious,
how chance can escape down a hole,
on the long lost slope of possibility.

Curious,
the tale of the male and the female.
Curious,
the tale of man and mouse.
Curiouser and curiouser,
the tale of you and me.
How we can open a window only to see
our tale escaping down the slope of eternity.

Nevermore, Nevermore, Nevermore

The clock strikes twelve.
The Cheshire Cat grins.
Oranges and lemons, say the bells,
at the circles we're in.
The hands tick round the clock.
The cat runs up to the top.
The clock strikes one,
the mouse runs down.
Down, and round, and out.

The clock strikes four.
It's time to pour, the tea.
Take milk, take sugar?
A china cup, a silver spoon.
Mother serving, children guzzling.
They giggle, as they wait for the riddle,
of raven, the ebony bird.

The clock strikes six.
Circle to the left, boys on the inside.
Circle to the right, and round about,
girls on the out.
Set to your partner,
clickety-click.

The clock strikes eight.
It's getting late. The cat is on the prowl.
The dog howls at the silvery moon.
Whistles of wind call, Lammermuirs.
Sierra Nevada, a mountain of snow.
Whispers, why did you go?
Circle to the left, circle to the right.
See how far you travel,
see how the line unravels.

The clock strikes twelve.
The cat has caught the ebony bird.
The mouse escapes, down and out.
The clock keeps turning, clickety-click.
To tour is not to travel.
To travel, arrive again,
like the raven who unravels time.
Time and again, he repeats, as he sings,
with his few notes,
Nevermore, Nevermore, Nevermore.

Orchid Hour

The cherry orchard flutters on the wind, its blossom blows the loss
of ages gone. The birds are voiceless, they no longer sing,
their eyes invisible, their feathers shorn.

A burning bush is greeting the return, its thorns are black,
its spikes are long. Seen through a darkened glass,
old hearts can learn, while cymbals tinkle, echoing our song.

Orchids are blooming, seen bright through glass,
so crouch in brambles, in dust and dirt. Voiceless, invisible,
beautiful lass, dandelions like suns, yellow alert.

Now midnight has rung, the clocks were all wrong.
Blossom has broken, the orchid is young.

Dog by the Pool

By Linn Rocks I lay down and slept,
the river a mirror below my head.
Martin's black Labrador sniffed me out
where noble artists painted the Pool.
On the High Street Square a little boy pees,
eternal fountain, an arc of wee.

Digi-Mining Kids are assembling - another legion of lego dogs.
The Labrador barks, feels his shadow escape.
He runs ahead - is captured, transformed, enslaved in a game.
Morphed, digital, pure data - his own double!
His hair has been harvested, his habits crafted, his memory mined.
His legs are like lego, his ego fine-tuned to yapp.
His ears prick up - a dog a picture!

Then Martin's black Labrador lifts his tail.
He sniffs the wind. His nostrils flare.
He exits the machine, leaps out through the window,
to join the little boy at the Fountain in the Square.

The Plough

The workhorse lays his head down,
his collar there against the ground.
He neighs and whinnies, one last time,
then looks up high, as clouds float by.
Around the edges shines the plough,
a field of stars, so bright that night.
He dreams he still is pulling hard.
He dreams he's strong and in his prime.
But no, this field is made of night,
a long dark one has just begun.
He shuts his eyes. He pricks his ears.
The plough shines on.

Prickly

The casket with the ashes jumped up,
hitting us between the eyes. A glass
between us, dark, with parallel half lives.
The ashes fly away. He'll curse us now.
Beyond the graveyard flows the river Styx.
Wild roses bloom and whin grows bright and thick.

Shit!

I'm not shouting, I'm screaming.
But they don't hear.

I crash my fist through the glass.

The veranda is smashed, they shout.
As I slink off to the woods.

Eucalyptus Tree

The wind is where I live. I dream it wild.
The leaves of this, my eucalyptus, wave,
so green and flowing; rolling thoughts
around, then down, along the wind.

The North Wind is not nice. It's made of steel.
It grins a chainsaw icicle, its smile,
and grins its teeth, afraid it might reveal
a softness or a warmth within.

The South Wind is a winner, on the wing.
It loves the summer when the air is warm.
It whistles in the trees and wakes the birds;
they flutter in the chorus, breaths of dawn.

My breath is where I live. My lungs are strong,
and when my eucalyptus tree is wild
I wave to it and thank it just for life,
for being there, and waving in the wind.

A Whisker Away

I walked into the room. The Passageway
to my bed was narrow. On either side
the books were piled, the papers high. My
kitten slept there, where lovers used to sleep.

"Miao" he said, then purring shut his eyes
and curled up, quite content. While I was left
to contemplate a pile of detritus,
remains of a life - projects half complete.

My resolution is to tidy up
quite soon. In fact tomorrow will do
for starters. And once I start I may not stop.
The whole house could go to the jumble sale.
But not my photos. I draw a line there.
They are the index. And my dead cat - alive still.

Under the Carpet

A flashing eye and fear of blindness. So
I visit Doctor Gentle. "Retina"
he says. Beware a dark curtain may
descend, and then you must go quickly, fast
to A and E, where they may operate.
Emergency! I watch each little light,
anxiety close, my nearest friend, while life
goes on, as if all were alright. And so
along with lost things, objects, things not done,
forgotten photos, a long dead mouse,
or a cool affront,
I shove it under my Persian carpet.

The Battle

In Durham Cathedral they ask me: Where are you from?
From Dunbar, I reply. Then they tell me: They buried them here.
The Scots soldiers, from the Battle of Dunbar.
The bodies are found of the men who marched South.

In Cambridge I ask, was it here? Was it here that Cromwell's
head is buried? They say yes, in Sydney Sussex College.
And my friend points to a room: where he stayed as a student.
He once was a young man too.

In Dunbar they speak of the battle, so many centuries ago.
Cromwell stayed in Broxmouth House, a wedding venue now.
Then horses charged in the moonlight. Men were slain by thousands.
The moon still shone over Doon Hill, and gannets flew around the Bass.

We could dig up the Scots, and move their bones home,
but their battle is no more. Their souls flew long ago.
They float like haar round Sula Bass Rock.
They shine like beacons in moonlit North.

Unexplained

Can someone please tell me the reason why
my silver bullets can kill off warlocks,
and bogles, whereas lead bullets just sink,
however hard I try.

Can someone please tell me the reason why
the Bass Rock, home to solan geese, soldiers
and saints, did not upturn when Tod Lapraik
the warlock came to die.

Can someone please tell me.
The answer came: "Not I."

January - The White Month

Volcano of foam, a wild sea; Winterfield.
A frothing creature, white and dangerous;
would eat you up. Its jaws are cavernous.
And it is jealous. Will it fight or yield?

It shows its teeth, and grins, a quiet smile,
on lips of waves, on breakers crashing rocks;
cement squares, left from wartime defense blocks.
The wrecks of ships are seen for miles and miles.

A polar bear is grinning wide, deep in water,
and swimming in Dunbar's wintry harbour.
It brought the foaming sea in too.
Its jaws could eat both me and you.

I see a mermaid with a tail of ice.
The polar bear is swimming by, with seals.
The pretty mermaid, fishy tail held high,
is in its mouth. In January, the whitest month.

The "Makar" Dunbar

His fear o death, an fear o a "drublie" winter
mak him jump oot the pages doon five centuries
tae land again on the Bass,
comin back on a boat frae France.

His fear o death, his "brukle" flesh
and his Dance of the Seven Deadly Sins
make me jump from my bed in quickness,
to no suffer frae "sweirness" o "Lichery".

Doon tae the kitchen I go,
glad to turn on Radio Four.
I throw sausages in the pan,
they sizzle just so.
Then up rises the "foul monstir Glutteny".

Crisscrossing My Skin

The lines on the map are clear.
Just north of Berwick on Tweed
lies the English border.
Here stops the heather.
Here you leave Scotland, for ever.

I first crossed that line at sweet seventeen.
A dizzy rock journey, girlfriends, hitching.
Edinburgh London, London Edinburgh.
Life-changing, crazy. Crazy life-making.

I crisscrossed that line many many times.
London, Liverpool, Cambridge, Newcastle.
North to south, South to north.
My compass swung, a pendulum.
A pigeon homing, rock dove returning.

In England I always knew
I was Scottish through and through.
I knew it with certainty, instinctual reality.
One dreamful day, fresh as desire,
lines crisscross, my face, my eyes.
I return for good, to my old country roots,
the warm log fires, the crocuses, the woods.

There as the wrinkles draw lines on my skin,
I remember the Thames, the Mersey, the Cam.
And the other Tyne - I was Hinny not Hen.
I loved those rivers, as the river of home.
The sound of their water is under my skin.

Long long will the heather bells ring.
The lines on the map are clear.
Just north of Berwick upon Tweed
you cross at the Scottish border.
There lies my old country - they now call Alba.
Here you may leave England,
but you are marked,
for ever.

A Castle in the Borders

Glorious golden the leaves on the way,
a glad and magic route down memory.
I become my grandmother, driving slowly,
time to watch the trees go by.

Castle turrets, and gargoyles in sun,
behind the lake in blue, gold-leaf trees.
Inside, the Setons, etcetera, and kin.
The ballad of four Marys on grandmother's lips.

Lady Alexandra, Sandy she was,
all fourteen years to my sixteen,
alone with her title in our frozen school dorms.
Where now? I ask. In Italy's warmth, perhaps.

So we all sip tea, by the fire, and admire
the pictures, layer on layer of amazing ancestors.
One was a rogue, and one was an artist,
one an Egyptologist, one spoke no English.

Yet century on century the first sons survive,
casting a few others to wars and disasters.
The blood-line intact; and just a few cracks
in the vast mirror with wood-carved frame.

In the warm wood-panelled room, the huge
mirror is especially wonderful, with flowers
placed below the cracks so perfectly,
hinting that perhaps, the Van Dyck is genuine.

This is a castle where you can believe. Here I hear
"Mary Seton, and Mary Beton, and Mary Carmichael,
and me." And grandmother Mary reciting them freely,
home once more from her wanderings, Egypt perhaps.

Home once more from afar and away,
home to the glorious lowlands of Scotland.
To see that picture of eternal golden leaves, and tea by the fire.
Glorious, with just the occasional crack, perhaps.

Dry Land

I'm anchored at last, the ship is home.
The world is crossed, the waves erased.
A plane has sunk below the ocean,
the deepest trench; no salvation.

Back home in Scotland, with wind and mud,
my dreams are crossed with sun and sweat;
the filth of Burma, its heavy heat,
where aching poverty hangs its head.

My bed is shaking; a train goes by.
The station a glimpse for weary travelers.
I wake from a dream on ocean waves,
the engine my mind, no ship in sight.

From here I travel in thought and word,
anchored firmly on dry land.
I freely roam, no fear, no filth.
The haar deep, my lilting heart.

But I hear deep, I feel the hurt,
of Myanmar, its fractured hand.
I'm happy, free, in dampest Scotland.
My dear, dreich, own land!

Humbie Kirk

High in the hills lies Humbie. Its kirk is hidden in a vale.
It hosts the hustings yet again, another election, the choice is ours.

A Holy House, earthly powers. A prayer to start, heckling later.
The questions tough, debate real. Humour and laughter, quite genteel.

In Humbie Kirk, so hidden away, the trials of the world seem quite unreal.
Scotland an Island within a sky, where snow in April can still defy
all expectation, all preparation, dropping like tears in this ancient vale.

Where choices crash from above like hail.

Scotland the Crazed

The rabble crowd is rampant and too loud.
The Saltires everywhere, bright blue and white.
They frighten me, all flapping as I pass.
Remind me of a dangerous bird, not paradise.

My Scotland has gone mad, it's like a crazy thing.
A prehistoric reptile come to life, its wings
emblazoned with a hundred badges.
Its name like machete -ism, or schism.

So here I sit all lost and cast adrift.
They call debate what I call hatred.
So, I want to fly away from here,
or just curl up and die, away from fear.
The nearest beach will do for me.
My head bent deep in sand, or bowed in prayer.

Celebration: Summer 2014

In Embra Town the festival is on.
The three week annual party has begun.
Its streets are bouncing; children with balloons
collide with clowns and fly on witches' brooms.

The Embra ale is alcoholic zest.
I sipped it in the Spiegel Tent, and yet
my head was split with poetry from New York
and referendum jokes from tartan Jocks.

We focus hard on books in Charlotte Square.
A famous guest is speaking when we hear
above, a mighty fly-by in the air,
and fire-works stuttering, loud, like gun-fire.
And blue saltires with their bright cross of white,
split through the middle, lighting up the night.

Next After the Twelfth

On the thirteenth floor of the Grand Hotel
an invisible door led to the river.
The Clyde was high; lights from the BBC
reflected brightly on the dark water.

Two policemen patrolled the cycle-path,
some unknown crime their midnight puzzle.
Two policemen pedalled back and forth;
a body lay under the Kingston Bridge.

Lorries thundered over the ten lanes,
crossing the river in the city centre.
The policemen stopped and interviewed
the drunk, the half drunk, and the sober.

The thirteenth time they passed under the bridge
an invisible lorry crashed the girders.

Pollok House, Glasgow

Sir William Stirling Maxwell went to Spain.
The Hapsburg jaw was dour as any Scot's.
While Phillip's mighty pen was writing lots,
Coello drew him; beard to hide his pain.

The library, a lady wrapped in fur;
El Greco's chiaroscuro, dark and bright;
her pink lips, black eyes, secret shining light;
her feelings, hidden down deep, move and stir.

A girl called Anne, in white dress, golden hair;
a baby lies awake in robes of kings.
They both are innocent, alive and free.
Jamaica, home to Maxwell slaves, its air
polluted, tainted, blood red bracelets, rings,
gave birth to art, through wealth; and we can see.

Fatrasie

Softest cheek pink chalk.
Hush now baby screeched the bird.

Softest cheek, pink chalk.
Parrot joke, don't squawk.
Bright baby, bright bird.
Pretty Polly talk.
Your form can not walk.
Your eyes are not heard.
My mother is hidden, scared.
Her voice comes out like a squawk.
A nightingale sings, is heard.
The painter's forms are soft chalk.
Hush now baby screeched the bird.

Melting Wax

The Rottweilers circle the main cathedral,
sniffing and barking, guarding their master.
A student strolls by, then walks much faster;
tough book in hand, he feels temperamental.

Back in his bedsit, young eyes scan pages,
Spanish syntax, "Señor Presidente".
Those who have nothing, those who have plenty;
terror the ghost who survives the ages.

High in the jungle the colibri sings;
the people eat maize seven days a week.
Down in the lakes, the tourist season brings
Swallow and Amazons, good food to eat.
Our student, now studies English Syntax:
Hollow men, innocence burnt, melting wax.

Straw Images

I see men of maize
in the jungle above.
I see men of straw
on the lakes below.
I hear hollow voices
talk of here and now.
I hear empty vessels
where a mother yells.

In Neruda's House

Young boy growing up, the Kingdom of Fife;
the Forth his river, the Lomonds his hills;
he breathed Scotland's blizzards, and winter chills;
as young man, he embraced a naval life.

Valparaíso, across many seas,
where the sun shines warm on Chile's long coast;
I could almost hear the commander boast,
in Neruda's house; gentlemen at ease.

"Almirante Cochrane", ship after ship;
the Chileans honoured him, naming thus.
Then past disgrace vanished, cup to lip;
Queen Victoria, a knighthood, lots of fuss.
Scotsman of the sea, retrieved from the past,
Lord Cochrane of Culross, is home at last.

King of Air

You sit astride a map of islands, Skye
and Uist, Barra. Winds from North
would take you high, your wings the length of tents.
Our guy ropes could not hold on Harris, so
we tied our house down. Maps and rope
will not restrain you, golden eagle, King
of Air; your beak will tell us stories high
and low, through salt and snow, sea and sleet.

You spy so many faces, wet in rain.
Old women, children; home fires grieving still
for Pict, or Celt; where Viking raiders burn.
Fresh blood with peat, mixed in the freezing wind.

From westward, exiles yearn, return
to Lewis, Harris, Uist, Barra, Skye,
from Canada, or Nova Scotia; east
to turquoise waters, silver sands, and death.

The northmost islands, Unst to Orkney, dark.
Norwegian words, their Viking forebears live.
Such tiny boats, on freezing oceans deep;
a fiddle tune aboard, peat fire back home.
The Sooth Mooth beckons sailors, long since dead,
and Lerwick seals are luring them to Shetland.

Highlands, magnificent, Suilven, Cairngorms.
The hillwalkers climb, the avalanche falls.
To Boat-of-Garten or Aviemore, skiers descend
from corrie, crag, through blizzard, snow.
So regal on peaks, the wild deer watching
while hunters crouch in the heather below.

Great raptor, King of Air, you see your prey.
Oh Golden Eagle, King of Birds, you see it all!

Linn of Dee

Sing April today, the coldest month, the thrush has cleared its throat,
while snow white melts, in rivers rushing. We relaxing, sun
on face, and Eliot's line, survives through time, an old
dear friend, in mind, not sight. The seven dwarfs ran off
and hid, but Snow-white survived, perennial, her long dress draped
over the mountain side, above Braemar, Moronne. Bright snow in April,
world is strange and plural, eternal. Cairngorms above, Heaven, the sky,
from Boat of Garten, skiing, the sheiling, to die in frost and ice, or time,
its face all lined like rocks from ages past, as generations rise and fall,
to stoop then stand again. Old cairns to mark the passage,
the seasons wanderings, as shepherd and sheep roamed, not lost,
just journeying. To every time its place, to every rhyme, its fine
to relax, enjoy the sun on face, the spring, the race,
to live, finally, to die. Today it is fine at Linn of Dee.

A Dale in the North

A vast oil terminal at Sullom Voe;
it crouches over Yell, a lunar beast.
Hear tales of lang sin syne, cutting peats,
prayers at white St. Magnus, Hamnavoe.

See Shetland ponies grazing, West Sandwick,
from Dale of Quam to Unst at Belmont House.
At Muckle Flugga see Stevenson's lighthouse,
St. Olaf's Kirk at Lunda Wick.

At Keen of Hamar lunar serpentine;
an MOD station, the highest hill;
a perfect viewpoint, skerries, northern lights.

The morn's morning, return to Lerwick time;
the haunted windhouse, an eternal chill;
we pass Mid Yell, Whalefirth on right.

Fresh eggs and bacon, butter, toast and jam;
a Shetland welcome, warmth and tunes, at Quam.

Raffle Prize

"No dogs in this carriage", said the train guard.
"Ah, but he's not a dog", I said, out loud.
While under my breath I whispered "Woa".
And clasped my hands round Woden's neck.

"Where's he from?" asked the woman opposite.
"He's a Yell baby", I answer her.
"Born on a bleak Wednesday night."
"Hell", said she. "Hide him under the table."

With one end each, we heave and haul him.
"Wednesday's child is full of woe".
The woman strokes him. Woden nuzzles her.
"He was born on a croft beside a Voe."

At St. Pancras the clatter of Woden's feet
drew stares and laughter, the children shrieked.
The tube was trickier, the escalator
a miracle of balance, an Oyster act.

In Brixton they thought the circus had come.
Maybe John Major would appear soon.
Woden was wonderful. Ears pricked, he pranced
in a Carribean Carnival dance.

In my daughter's garden we let him loose
by the fox hole under the apple tree.
He ate the grass, and swished his tail.
A long way from Shetland and that fateful raffle.

The Unforgiving Island

The crisp air of Braemar crystallized the start. Skeleton Island,
what a thrill! Long John Silver, a Spy Glass Tavern.
Pirates, drunkenness, glorious treasure. The Hispaniola,
and a bottle of rum, in the unforgiving Caribbean.

The humid air of Haiti. A wisp of hair a memory.
A city struck, an island quakes, skulls are cracked
and bodies break. Skeleton Island, the word made bone.
Hispaniola, no morphine, no rum. In the unforgiving Caribbean.

Anstruther

A garden in the sea.
Waves crash.
The Bass Rock, back to front
on the horizon.
Berwick Law reversed
in landlocked mirror.
A Derek Jarman Style of Art -
this gallery garden.
Ceramics, cairns, mirrors, rocks.
But always the distant howling
of waves,
leaping closer as time ticks
its inevitable
seconds, minutes, years, eons.
The rocks crash down,
old foundations,
built on sand.
They crack, crumble,
like bones.
Waves rule
on this old herring shore.
Elderly friends climb steep steps,
their minds on conceptual art.
The waves rule,
as always before.
When the storm comes,
the perfect storm,
the really big one,
then waves chase waves,
crash over, under, through
the side of their home
and the perfect view.
When the wolf waves come hunting,
there is nowhere to hide
from its claws of foam.

The Rock

Cleft from ages,
left for all.
Guano like bones,
a heart of stone.

Fly close seabird,
touch the wall.
Your cry is heard,
its fleeting call.

Cross the door,
touchstone of yore.
Sula bassana,
so long Solan.

Remarkable Rocks

The Isle of May is basalt. The Bass a phonolite plug.
Volcanic rocks, enduring.

The Terns on the Isle were dive-bombing, heading straight for my eyes
like knives. I lowered my cap to fill the gap, my glasses remained intact.

By Borough Market my grandson plays, a square by Southwark Cathedral.
Chasing pigeons, running for fun. Enduring friendship, the shining sun.

Years like rocks, glinting; granite submerged, then visible.
Cruiser boats, the River Thames; a big red bus from London Bridge.

Crowds that day, in Borough Market, but kindness. A male stranger
helps with our heavy pushchair. The Shard sharp in the background.

Friendship, love, the sun, persist. The Bass Rock of home is fixed, invisible,
but present in the mind's eye. Gannets swirling on the wing, screaming.

You'd Never Believe Me ... But ...

A bag can be the mirror of the soul.
Newton, who measures the world with his compass
could not encompass the sphere in total.
The circle is squared in Bloomsbury's gaze.

You'd never believe if I explained.
Awakened by Waves on the rim of my mind.
A room of my own my only ambition.
Virginia Woolf, a chloroform stream.

From Chemistry to consciousness,
her influence real, still, the turning.
Then typing, Southampton Row.
Strolling down Great Russell Street.

Sleeping in a Women's Hostel.
Diana Ross and the Supremes
singing from the record player.
Right-on books. Leicester Square.

Decades leap and Goodge Street looms.
Growing high, UCL Hospital.
The Middlesex pulled down, all rubble.
There used to be a tunnel.

Foley Street, where I worked, and swam.
A swimming pool in the old nurses' home.
The Brunswick, for films and noodles.
Judd Street, the books on my commute.

The British Museum, once my neighbour,
when I was less than twenty.
I'll take my grandson there one day,
son of my dear darling daughter.

A little girl drawing, sitting on my knee,
in that inclement town by the North Sea.
Creator of the British Library Bloomsbury bag.
Yes, a beautiful bag can mirror the soul.

The Sun High

The train draws in to Leuchars,
twenty five years gone down the line.
The platform where my girl
aged two, aged four,
jumped about in excitement,
an excursion to Edinburgh.

Today I head for Dundee.
The Tay stretched out
in the February sun
as beautiful as in 1986.
Light dancing on the lapping waves,
heralding another spring time,
close as water.

My daughter paddling
on St. Andews beach,
twenty yards from our house.
The sun high in the sky,
a bright summer.
And I didn't lose her in Dundee,
the deep crowds.
But one day we left
Leuchars station for ever,
like the jets, flying high.

A First

A first trip to Wimbledon with the push-chair.
I plan it carefully. It takes me hours.
From Herne Hill to Wimbledon Chase is one journey.
Easy!
From Herne Hill to Wimbledon Station is two.
I could change at Mitcham Junction.
But does it have a lift?
Or I could carry on to Wimbledon Chase,
and then catch a bus,
or even walk.
I consult Google Maps.
How far, I wonder is it?
I see 22 minutes
beside an icon of a walking man.
That may be me.
I like to walk,
and if the road is not a busy highway
I will take the low road.
Perhaps!
There is still more research to do
on this new journey.
With my grandson, aged two,
to meet, for the first time,
his sort-of grand-aunts.

Spring to Autumn - Faces in Time

Spring-1981:

The Cliffs of Dover glinted white, spring
in our steps and in our eyes. Twin rings
gleaming like smiles. The ferry spray,
our faces splashed with foam, such fun.
Each day a journey, no-where booked.
Paris - a mystery. Life as life comes.
Changing my name - casually.
Merging my identity.
A moment captured on old fashioned film.

Autumn-2019:

The brambles are over, rotting on the bush.
Summer has gone. Autumn is golden.
Rosehips are splendid, orange and bright.
Roadside apples sour. Garden apples sweet.
I spot some red berries in our local wood.
I wonder, could I try them, how would they taste?
I pop the leaves and the fruits in a little pot.
My friend's phone has a fancy plant app.
She instantly identifies them.
Woodland Nightshade and Yew. Both deadly.
I put the app on my own gadget,
so I can capture in images my garden plants.
It requests access to all my photographs,
where my infant grandsons' faces live.
I deny access.
I will wander the woods,
observing the details of the leaves
testing and tasting in the old fashioned way:
taking life as life comes.

Hum Drum

Bees buzz around the purple rose.
Insects sun themselves on nettle stalks.
Tourists burn their necks, their toes.
Turquoise seas, boats, a dolphin talks.

High in the hills I hear the drums.
An army of bumblebees humming.
Honey is sweet from the mountain rose.
Nettles and stick insects clicking.

Clap clap go the castanets.
Clickity click, beat faster yet.
Hum hum buzz the bumble bees.
Drum drum, beats my heart's ease.

Scarborough

The fair is calling, come along and dance.
The sea is calling, mermaids swimming deep.
The cliffs are falling down, while people sleep;
casinos buzzing; come and try your chance.

A breakfast by the pier, coffee, sunshine,
and donkey rides; a beach of children's smiles.
A man does handstands; arms with huge muscles.
The tourists queue to laugh, and spend, in line.

In campsites full of mud the people crowd
to drink in dismal bars, vodka and beer.
Relentless music pumped; there's no escape.

In memory the horses circle round,
and mermaids' sounds are ringing in your ear
to lure you back, far back; the fair is great!

The Red Shed

The lupins in the garden led the way
and pots of compost, leaves, a multi- green
and red, melange, a brighter better day.
The shed the very best I've ever seen.

Inside the door, ajar, the hinges creek.
I wait to see surprises in the air.
Imagination leaps, or skims my cheek,
with winter robin landing, red on chair.

Oh Lady, please, please put your spade just here,
beside the fir tree. I can sit on it.
Together thus, and you can brush your hair.
That biscuit bar - I'll have a bit of it!

I like the snow behind, said hoppity.
A perfect photo opportunity.

Yellow Aconites

I bring the white hot anger in my heart.
I place it on the winter window sill.
I hope by springtime it has blown away,
become a snowdrop white as Christmas stars.

I bring the red hot anger in my head.
I place it on the fireplace by the stove.
I hope by summer it becomes dry ash;
gone out. Its hot red thoughts a babbling thrush.

In January outward I will go,
along lost footpaths where snowdrops grow.
There I will search for yellow aconites,
and later, crocuses, with white flowers;
or even purple. And I will bury anger there;
forget-me-nots blooming, a thrush nearby.

Millennium Friends

Scattered like snowdrops, through winter gardens,
the yellow aconites all around.
The agony of yesterday, heralding spring,
the roots have spread far, tomorrow the crown.

Scattered like raindrops, through distant harbours,
with purple butterflies all around.
The chaos of yesterday, heralding sunshine,
the beat of their wings on the rainbow of time.

Scattered like stars, from a ten year eruption,
I look to the heavens, for yule-tide lights.
I see my friends watching, a million eyes waiting,
like teardrops or snowdrops, a new decade to start.

Little Flower

Blue, you sadly droop. Blue, you glorious look.
Blue, you drink the brook. Dropping dew, you ring your bell.

For fairies the bell tolls, not humans, the story tells. Woodland
carpet, rustic enchantment. Ring gently scented, of jewels like lilies.

A hyacinth family awaits to embrace thee.
Love everlasting, an emblem, an aching.

In spring you surface, bright from dark earth,
cyan, pink, purple, you gather and circle.

A bonny belle, a fairy thimble,
alive and gracious, slender and nimble.

Blue in your beauty, blue in your glory.
In sunshine and sorrow, a circle of bluebells.

The Lost Hour

Winter is over. It's time for summer.
Move the hour forward. Remember, remember!

The weekend is shorter. I want it longer.
Summer hours are lighter, less burdensome and brighter.

In autumn I'll recover the hour I lost in spring.
The penalty is darkness, and winter will begin.

If all our hours could be exchanged,
each minute swapped for warmth,
with every second we'd be changed.
A lost hour a chance for growth.

Growing It

My garden is muddy.
Tangled.
In summer the wild strawberries
wind around the base of my roses.
A hawthorn bush gives shelter to birds
feeding on nuts and seeds.
In springtime baby sparrows flop and flutter.
In winter I spy a robin, and a wren,
waiting their turn.

There's a long "To Do List" for the digging
and the tidying.
But I prefer to potter about,
plant a few bulbs, pick a few daisies,
forage for apples, and rosehips.
My wildlife garden is messy, but fun.

I fear the bullets pointing at my hedgehogs.
My prickly friends should not be roasted.
They should feel free to explore my strange jungle.

My garden of memories is also muddy and tangled.
But I muddle through.

ENDINGS

Elemental Airs

The Celebration was vibrating all over the valley.

They had come from the North, where the whale's road leads West.
They had come from the South, where the sun sets on deserts.

The bands were playing, the bagpipes crying.
Drums were thumping, children jumping.
Great groups gathering. A Celebration!
Only the dreaming guitar was weeping.

Some came on horseback from youthful valleys.
Some swam in from the sea with rafts.
Some on the steam trains, came puffing and huffing.
Others on reindeers from Lapland, with magic.

She knew them all, embraced them all.
But the ones she missed most
came over the hills, out of the mists.

And when they returned, surreal, funereal,
to the air where they lived, to the morning mind,
as the dream faded, she chased them wildly,
mourning and forlorn.

Cynthia's Nearly Sixty Sonnets

I'm nearly sixty, fifty eight or nine.
I've lived so long, I leave a string of wrongs.
My errors line up, turning into songs,
or slip away to beam a smile, sun-shine.

I love the rhythm, fourteen lines; an hour-
glass world of syllables, of joys and hates;
old memories of Herbert, Donne, and Yeats;
then Shakespeare, seven ages, summer's flower.

So sixty sonnets, nearly done. I've now
grown older still, but yet my pen will trace
the lines upon my face, and mirror how
I drew some jokers, ones and twos. But Ace
of Diamonds waited in the wings, its spark
of light eternal, fortunate and sharp.

A Party Fit for Gods

My eucalyptus down, the gale unknown,
my garden reeling, plants not flowering yet.
A picnic table smashed, the weight too great.
Its wood was rotten, old, frail, done.

Yet nature can be challenged, blown away.
A party fit for Gods on holiday
was sparkling, fizzing, popping corks, all day,
ideas circling, joyous company.

So sixty years and cycling onwards still,
my youthful past a dream, the future more.
Old friends and new, my tented garden full,
all looping, leaping, time, the past before
and after. Daughter, son-in-law,
my cousins, brothers. Cambridge in Dunbar.

Hopping

The toads are hopping, jumping over roads.
Their pond is brimming, water, weeds: it's home.
They go together, in groups, not alone,
but cars and lorries squash them: heavy loads.

The Binning Wood, a graveyard, trees and deer.
Organic bodies, earth to earth, all green.
Newbyth beside it; fast a road between.
They're going home, then crack; their cries we hear.

So March has come; the time has come to spawn.
A knot of toads is croaking by the pond.
They grew as tadpoles here, so know it well.
In winter, sleeping under logs and stones,
through cold and ice they hibernated long.
'Til happy, hopping, crash, they enter Hell.

Global Gulls

Voices, shrill, like gulls - of the invaders - shriek.
Layers upon layers of lost memories
linger in the frosty air. Those long gone
from this beloved beach look on as from a deep sleep,
as Londoners speak of leverage and derivatives,
in what was once our winter wilderness.
Close by we came with mother and grandmother
to picnic in summer, not a soul to be seen.
Do they watch us now, our anchored ancestors?
Do they wonder as we wander unanchored,
like ships astray on a global highway?
Do they hear the gulls shriek -
where once there was silence?

Cove in the Rocks

Semi-circular chamber, cut deep in the rocks.
Red gems, sandstone beach, a soft hand-up.
Mountainous rock to climb upon -
children laugh scarlet, vermilion.
Shine bright in sun, under January's veil.
Reveal far-off features, threads of cinnabar.
Curves like bodies, shoulder blades in waves.
A hand from the past, to forever caress.
Behind lie Lammermuirs, ahead the North Sea.
Church bells are heard, in the caves with the surf.
Geology's arches, etched from long years.
Eyebrows and glances, gestures, leap years.
Erosion, formation, eternity swells.
Echoes from ancestors, the old Craig-en-Gelt.
Courting and laughter, froth in the ripple.
Tide waits for no-one, the centuries roll,
so rejoice and embrace the old push and pull.

Beyond the Black Rock

First shortbread, coffee, chat, the RLS
Club gathering. North Berwick ready; sun
shines; sea gleams; walking history begun
by Blackadder's gravestone; on Kirk Ports. Yes!

We pass the Quadrant; on Marine Parade
we stroll, the Bass Rock tilted skywards; then
the black rock rises; Stevenson and friends
once climbed there; childhood verses, sun and shade.

An outing to the farm, a spellbound trip,
to Auldhame, wrecker countryside; Seacliff
nearby, and Scoughall, where Mrs. Dale once lived;
and memories of cousins, horses, ships
at sea, and Solan geese; then Colinton,
a Manse. Ancestors call from far beyond.

Ancestors

All gather here, the kirk is full once more,
as decades wind back, fifty, ninety. So,
we sing, we pray, we bury, as before,
the generations spinning, top to toe.

But gone with them the etiquette of death,
where each one knew the role they must play out;
the final dance, macabre, now fettered;
the solemn walk of black, today greyed out.

So long lost cousins greet and meet again,
and laughter follows coffin to the grave.
I see our fathers disapprove. What shame!
And we discuss the long gone ones, who gave
us genes, which make us look alike; chose
ancestors' names.
                                        The shape of our children's nose.

Déjà Vu

Swallows over the dunes,
Déjà Vu.

Peffer Burn a trickle,
sandy too.

Hollows echo old tunes,
ancient view.

Keats heard the nightingale
singing through

centuries, or eons,
false or true.

Up and down, hill and dale,
me and you,

feasting still, meat and ale.
Time breaks through.

Our paths are cyclical.
Two by two.

Spirit or animal,
both are due

in the ark, animate,
there to woo.

Boat on a sandy lake,
currents too.

He held his hand to take
her hand too.

Adam spied Eve, amputate,
part of you,

your rib, then copulate.
One is two.

Pain, pleasure, both can make
humans true.

Pleasure, pain, both remain,
shifting dunes.

Hollows echo old games,
sing our tunes.

Adam, Keats, other names,
long eons.

Different but the same,
sing cuckoo.

Chords of the nightingale
vibrate true.

Eternal, cyclical,
I and you.

Time vanishes, owls hoot,
wits to woo.

Darkness on the Peffer Burn.
Déjà Vu.

Etched in the Sun

The wind in the trees,
the wasps in the sun,
the bees hum a lullaby,
crushed are the plums.
The gate to the garden
a grail wrought of iron,
a maze all the summer -
paths through peas,
peach and vine.
It was there we would wander
searching glorious light,
an endless wander-land,
our rabbits in sight.

Then crash went the bulldozer,
bang went the crane,
improvement and progress
the grail of our age.
Machinery of harvest,
dryer of grain,
a monster robust,
a vast gaping wound.
It whirred and it burst,
between and behind,
wound its tentacles round,
the sweet shoots of the vine.
Sea-monster from Hell
this Leviathan.

So the rabbits went running,
the beast broke their backs.
The tunnels were filled in,
the air turned jet black.
This garden of Eden
ripped right out by the root,
from its ashes arose
a great puff of grey smoke.
And the grain from the dryer,
fresh bread from the land,
the green fruits of Eden
impressed in the sand.

The green minds of childhood
climb and grow like the vine.
The small thoughts of children
smoke and burn through all time.
When the grail of the garden
turns to rust, rough and brown,
the maze where the wasps hum,
is still etched in the sun.

Revisiting

The track is still there, blocked off maybe,
but the quarry is there, where my cousin and I camped,
he deep under ground now,
we, so many years ago, teenagers, young in spirit,
get up and go, afraid of nothing, knowing nothing,
camping, all weekend, an adventure to be called
mother of all.

Above, in the trees, reaching high, lies the ruin,
where falling towers and broken steps are held with ivy,
close, to stop them falling,
close, to keep an old family warm,
here on the cliff top, looking down,
an iconic image their view,
iconic now, but remote as dawn
in that earlier time
when snowdrops clumped by the doorway
or in little vases on the stair,
the only sign of life.

Where did they go then?
The children who lived here.
Did they sail through the winter fog
past the roar of the horns
or await the shimmering summer sea?
Did they kiss and run away, or kiss and marry?
And their mother,
did she rejoice that they were free?
Or did she lie down in her bride's veil
with her head buried in the cold sand?

The sea is lapping around the cliff,
the church bells ring where snow drops grow.
Spirits are talking in the ancient wood,
old conversations heard as new.
A matriarch with lines on her face,
criss-crossing like well-worn paths,
is talking to children, their duty, their place.
She loves them. Will she let them go?

They may go by sea, they may go on horse-back,
they may walk or run or swim or ride.
But sure as the tide comes lapping, at the cliff edge,
they will come visiting again, in youth
and again, in age
revisiting again, and again
for all time.

A Glimpse of Mountains

A view of Suilven; sun high, air in breath;
its saddle tight; a galloping at pace.
As mists drop ghostly shrouds, and shifting shapes;
chiaroscuro, changes; bracken, heath.

A pebble thrown, its ripples grey on loch,
or river; waves, and horses chasing white,
chalk lines through time; our pictures dark and light,
from castle, dungeon, clearings, ruins, broch.

Near Durness, rocks are pink with human face,
and caves are open under normal ground.
Loch Naver, remember, our pebbles lost;
a mountain glimpsed, which I can never chase.
A photo captures moments, joy and sound.
Both Sugarloaf and Suilven, now are ghosts.

The Lines on Your Hand

Silicon from sand, like blood from stone,
the lines on your hand are not yours alone.
After all these years, after all this time,
the lines in your mind are not yours but mine.

Breast to breast, bones to bones, day by day, clay to clay.
Silicon chips, short circuit brain, hard wired electricity.
My brain a wafer-thin circuit, mercurial memory.
Semiconductor mind, electrical energy. I draws life from you.

Dust to dust. Sand to sand. Silicon, "con amor",
love conquers all. The lines on your hand are not yours alone.
Those lines are hard-wired in my mind and my bones.

Wrecks

How the ship lay,
gasping its last,
its rasping breath
as on a death bed.
Grasping at the wreck,
rowing or drowning,
bodies and souls strove
to survive, to remain alive.
The ship at Dunbar's shore,
memories of a Ravensheugh wreck,
that picture in our living room,
from childhood's imagination.

Those tales told by my Aunt Lucy
of the wrecks and their booty.
Were the lights shone to lure
poor souls to the shore?

Another life was wrecked
on the ridgebone reefs,
with no harbour in site,
just a river,
a long way from the sea,
with a bridge,
and a marriage,
too rigid to resist
the creeks and the cracks
of the wood as it splintered,
of the ship as it sank.

Behind

We kiss so gently under the ghostly moon.
Your eyes drown mine as fast as the sea.
My heart ebbs slowly as waves in nets.
Your wake is cast, in a line behind.

Crossroads

The large ship crossed in front,
leaving its wake.
My rowing boat rocked from side to side,
feeling the pulse.

Foam crossed foam,
white roads in water.
In the distance you were waving,
the whale's road your laughter.

Your hand stretched out,
an eager farewell.
My hands clasped close,
in the watery swell.

Your smile was wide,
as you crossed the tide.
Your wake a dirge,
a pulse of sorrow.

Our Last Night

Our Sold Sign is up,
Our time is up.
Our home is living on borrowed days.
I live here alone.
My daughter comes home
For a last night.
We have supper with friends,
Old friends, a soul supper.
We met when I was young,
Now I am old.
My house is sold.
The last supper is over.
We drank to the past,
We drank to the future.
No one mentioned a cock crowing,
Or a sour supper of yesteryear.
No one dwelt on the tears of the past
Or the absent one who unites us like a ghost.
We laughed and laughed so as not to cry,
And our souls sang, and will sing on,
So as not to die,
Long past the unknowable dawn.

Words and Silence

In between the soul
somewhere flaps its wings
and tries to sing
but the notes fall like feathers
to the floor.
I see an open door
flapping in the wind
as it creaks on its hinges
and swings to and fro.
So life goes.
We try to speak
but our voice is not heard
above the din
of the doors on their hinges
and the flapping and the clapping
of other poor souls
whose shrill calls
cry out and try to touch,
in the whistling of the storm.
In its eye.
Is it you, is it I,
that I hear calling
that I see falling?
Let us try to float
gently like a feather.
Let us land softly close
to the soul of the wind
somewhere serene
between words and silence.

Remembrance: 1914 - 2014

A field of poppies, all ceramic red.
A crowd of mourners gather round the bed
of flowers. Youth, its blood all fierce and spilt
where it should run through veins with love again.

The generations flow; they come, they go.
At thirteen years a boy becomes a man
and soon he will be fit for work, or war,
and like great uncles round the world

he will be fit to die. His country needs
him, so they say. His sister too, and she
would always wish he'd stayed to scythe the corn
in poppy fields back home, where he was born.
She wished his blood of pumping youth could run,
and breed like rabbits; hop, and leap the sun.

The Bluebell Track

Wild garlic, white and smelly, bluebells thick;
red campion, poppies; blood, at Flodden's field.
A bright blue sky, all crossed in white; in ink
the red of England's flag, like mud we yield.

At Swanston cottage blooming flowers, youth.
A writer breathed the Pentland air, Glencorse.
The young man's lungs lost breath; then came ill-health.
His pen, a knife, engraved; head, hands, and corpse.

So flowers of Scotland, Flodden, Stevenson,
the sun of June is bright, but mud is deep.
Our crosses can be white or red, or black.

With blue above, and bright the loyal sun
in Heaven; walk our ancient paths with sheep;
Keep straight ahead; go chase the bluebell track.

Autumn Spirits

In Highgate Cemetery the leaves are red;
Karl Marx's grave a tourist magnet spot;
a path with cyclamens, where bodies rot;
George Eliot at peace; her petal bed.

The spirit lives; Virginia Woolf afloat
upon October breeze; her father rests
a little up the hill; while other famous guests
make way for statues, moss, roots; their words flowed.

In Highgate Cemetery the ivy climbs
so green and high; Karl Marx's giant head
below, uniting workers. Music chimes,
and harmony, for Mahler's daughter, dead;
her sculptured hands held high, her hidden face;
while trees look down; and Christ, his cross in place.

Birdsong and Drums

A funeral breeze whistling.
Young girls laughing,
from Aurthur's Seat to Leicester Square.
Our youth a whim, without a care.

A funeral sound booming.
Young girls dancing,
from jazz at six to blues at ten.
Our youth a waltz, without the drums.

A lone piper plays on.
Young girls grown old.
From jazz and laughter, to birdsong.
Alone, we hear the distant drums.

Crumbling

I arrive early, before the crowds reach Edina.
The sun is bright on the gardens,
the sky blue.
The castle looms on my left.
I glimpse the pillars of St. Cuthbert's Church.
Wander over, explore the graves,
looking for De Quincey.

I see a sign:
Two eminent men are buried here,
Napier of Logarithmic fame
and De Quincey, an Author.
But tourists may also look
for Burke and Hare
among the eminent ghosts found here.
Not yet seventy I still walk well,
but the path is treacherous.

At seventeen,
having lurched from an ancient girls' school,
I drifted up at Napier Tech.
Studied physics and physical sciences
and embarked on a voyage with multiple purposes.
Much later in an ancient English library
I read De Quincey's multiple volumes
compiled by a dead Edina professor.
His version of Judas Iscariot washed up
in an old Argentine essay,
and mine surfaced in an eNote.

I wander over, before the festival crowds,
past the crumbling mausoleums,
on the paths as instructed,
because of the danger of stone slabs falling:
Searching for Thomas De Quincey.

After the Show

A savage start,
with a climb on the Pyrenees.
In my mind!
Then a hard pavement on George Street
rose up to meet me.
Bang!

My Adam's rib crushed between
Spain and Edinburgh.
A solid book dangling,
to break the Fall.

My elbow sharp,
like those death bends on the road
in Iran.
I headed overland to India on Budget Bus,
aged twenty.

My elbow crushed, like freedoms.
So hard to win, so quick to lose.

In Toledo, Spain's Transition,
Democracy dawns.
Our glorious view over the Cigarrales.
On television the hooded hordes in black.
Iran, Khomeini.

In Liverpool, the Inner City,
hard, but free.
My anger rose at Hillsborough,
and the Burning of the Books.

At the end of the show,
in Charlotte Square,
I stumbled upon Salman Rushdie.
A no-show ticket,
landed by chance in my lap.

When asked about "The Satanic Verses"
and the Ayatollah,
Rushdie replied:
One of us died, but it wasn't me.

Arthur's Seat

What kind of erupting volcano were you to do what you did do?

At Salisbury Crags you jumped, they say, over the edge.
What edge were you on, to jump that day, to erupt that day,
like a lion that has lain dormant for too long.

You extinguished your lamp, like the Lady of Shalott,
when all the Knights of Camelot crossed themselves for fear.
What precipice did you cross? What cross did you bear,
that bipolar death day that precipitated you here .

What kind of extinct volcano were you to do what you did do?

Muted

We walk the river; broom or whin. The win
was exit, leave. I voted stay, remain
within the European family.
The wild pink rose my favourite flower in bloom.

The others stride ahead along the path.
The boats are moored nearby, along the edge,
the other side. I walk alone, the rain
begins to fall, its drops like tears pour down
my cheeks. And dreams of youth are mute as swans.
And hopes of youth, the wild pink rose, are gone.

We place a casket in the ground.
Another life is over, one who crashed
our family like a plane, just landing where
he pleased, with no thought how or why or what.
It's over now, the past and all it brought.
The wild rose by the river will wither soon.

Iron Bite

In the bleak mid-winter.
we are all alone.
Families fight like cocktails,
sticks and stones and bones.

Snow I love and ice waves,
crashing by the beach.
Family fighting freezes me,
frosty blood, iron bite.

Freedom from this mill stone,
let it slip away.
Melt to water with the dawn,
drip or drop or drown.

Like a spirit I have wished,
to gently slip away, to canter
carefree down the beach,
careering as we play.

Let's have a party on the rocks,
let's rock and roll, and lay down.
Like Auld Lang Syne let's raise a glass,
again some winter's day long.

Stronsay

The deep-breathing sea,
sound of tranquillity.
Silver sand or summer ring,
seals submerged,
unknown depths.
Waves and prayers,
lapping gently.
Wings and feathers,
flapping, chirping.
Silence is broken,
your word is spoken.
May your will be done,
may we not be undone.
Waves to waves,
water to water.
A ring of white wishes
like lambs to the slaughter.
Breathe deeply blue sea,
hear the sounds of tranquillity.
Let the silver wishes fly,
freed from care,
to the sky.

"Of Manis Mortalitie"

"Lyk as ane shaddow in ane glas", William Dunbar

The child in the mirror himself he sees.
A moment of opportunity.
Himself, another, his own, his double.
He's toil and trouble, but joy and jubilee.

He jumps for light, chases his shadow.
His head in the clouds.
Heart in the middle.
His feet are running, racing Achilles.

The mirror ticks, it's six o'clock.
The sundial stops, its's ten past ten.
The shadow lengthening, the mirror cracks.
Ice opens its hands, and grasps his feet.

The ferryman lurks, the river flows.
The fee is due, for folly past.
The ghosts are ashen, waiting near.
The mirror cracks, becomes broken glass.

Call the Ferryman

Ferry 'cross the Channel.
The wind blew in our hair.
The sun shone. We kissed.
The photo remains the same.

Ferry 'cross the Mersey.
New Brighton in sight.
The twist, wild. My four year old.
She loves you Yea Yea.

Ferry out of Lerwick.
Seals crying on Sooth Mooth,
Remember other ferries. I wretch.
Behind my eyes sharp seal tears lurk.

The ferryman lingers, the river flows.
The fee is due at last.
The ghosts are ashen, waiting near.
The mirror cracks, becomes broken glass.

A Place to Go

I came to be with my family.
What did I end with?
The Sea.

Its constancy,
its motions,
like an old friend.

Always there,
I start to rely
on its moods.
Its fair weather or foul.
A place to go.

"Oh, let's go down to the sea today".
Its tides will welcome me.
No tea or coffee, but
its salt taste on my tongue,
its damp kiss on my lips,
its open air embrace,
its being just that,
the sea.

Shimmering on the Edge

On my lookout post I survey the Isle of May.
A school trip, a distant memory.
My bike propped up by Dunbar Golf Club,
waves lap around the rock I am on.
Sun on the wave, sound of the sea,
these are all I need, they are Heaven to me.
The water circles, the rivulets form.
The same pools surround me, it's Seacliff, 1960.
My mother calls, my cousins run,
Diana, Joanna, such fun, such fun.
This is eternity, my self my own company.
But reality incessantly, floods, unfortunately.
The pressure is rising, the waves are crying.
Return, return, though you sleep on dry land.
Return to the water, return to the sea,
to the long endless summers when we all were so wee.
When we all were so innocent, so tender and free,
when the winds made the horses toss their harness and neigh.
On my lookout post, I survey the lost Isle of May.
It shimmers on the edge, where the sky meets the sea.
Its spire points up to Heaven, its base is on the earth.
It lies on the horizon, as a beacon from the past.
I hope one day to reach it. I hope one day to know.
It is rising and resplendent, like the ones who went before.

Galloping to the End

If I could revisit the smiddy
where I smelt the burning hooves,
the clatter of iron on iron,
good shoes for galloping.

I would smell the horse manure,
feel flies buzzing in the hot afternoon,
hear the gentle whinny, our recognition,
my chestnut mare, bright as the rowan.

If I could revisit
the smell of burning hooves,
and feel the clattering of iron galloping,
then the wild wind would be in our nostrils
and we would charge the waves,
united in mythical adventure.
Any fall an amputation.

I am at primary school
at the vet's last visit.
My dead mare,
childhood's obituary.

Red-Hot

Embers, glowing red, bright on snow.
Roses, by the window, pink on green.
On the TV:-
A polar bear pup, sucking milk.
Plastic baubles in water, bottled pollution.
On the wall the clock has cracked.
Time ticks backwards.

Chile-pepper curry, red-hot.
Carrot and coriander, squash soup.
Snow outside, not so inside.
On the TV:-
Cold air in the breath of the Beast from the East.
Bacon breakfast in Daddy's kitchen.
Partial paralysis, the lungs shut down.

A white horse on a chalk plain.
Lime etched in time.
Secrets near by in Porterhouse Down.
Old witch alchemy stirring her cauldron,
due process her watchword.
Mix red-hot sticks with glinting icicles.
"Respect Chemistry" written on her wall.
Strive for the quicksilver solution
to the puzzle of the Cold Haar.

Red-hot irons on the horses' hooves.
A smell of burnt protein.
Flesh in the air, feet like nails.
After breakfast in Daddy's kitchen
we galloped on the chalk plains
free as the seagulls in from the coast.
At Dover the cliffs are even whiter
than the song remembered.
The musty smell of horses' breath
hung in the air, like a hologram.
And horses' sweat entered our skins
like the red-hot summer sun.

We lunched in the Fizzy Restaurant
by the bay window,
where the roses in the crystal vase
were pink on green.
We hid our faces as someone passed.
We had not been seen.
We sipped red wine.
Our tongues were hot, with talk

Blood-red Robin and Blackbird in the Bleak Night

In this dark dank January my sparrows hope for spring.
They flutter, a great flock, rising from my bushes as I pass.
I grew their home, and feed them seeds and nuts.

From time to time they are joined in their foraging
by a robin, a wren, or a blackbird, who also live here.
Sometimes a pigeon, a sea-gull, or a squirrel visits.

They brighten my mood in the dark winter
and I comfort myself, hoping to truly belong
within the tangled web of winter survival.

Meanwhile, I await spring,
when the black bird will sing,
doing my little bit.

Easier than giving blood.

Red on White

In the week of the Bleak Mid-
when the snow lies low on the hills.
We will go with King Wen-
 where the frost lies in its den.

In the howl of the cruel ice
we'll hear the Halleluyas,
and Christ will come to save our
Souls. As sinners we rejoice.

In the garden the robins sing
their breasts red as holly.
They feed on nuts like humble
sparrows, but they are little Gods.

In this week of the Bleak, red wine
is the colour, red on white.

Witnessing a Ghost

The spare room was where the ghost stayed.
The spare room was at the top of the stairs.
The little girl rushed past the room and down the stairs.
"I can't sleep," she said.

"The moon is asleep," said her mother.
The little girl crept up the stairs, each step creaking.
At the top of the stairs, she turned the corner
past the room where the ghost stayed.
It was dark, navy dark, as the moon was asleep.
Later that night the moon crept out from the sky
and it shone its light into the spare room,
where the ghost lived.

Later, many decades later,
the girl stayed in the spare room.
When she looked out of the window,
there was the moon.
And in its arms she saw her mother.
The moon was a cradle.
Its light shone bright.

The Lights of Home

Nineteen seventy seven, in our sleep.
All the lights went out, one by one, by turns.
Darkness and shadows overwhelmed the deep.

Pilgrimage, Whitekirk, our mother to weep.
In Heaven a daffodil candle burns.
Nineteen seventy seven, in our sleep.

Fragile flames flicker, a twenty year leap.
Ely Cathedral, all chanting in turns.
Darkness and shadows overwhelmed the deep.

Daffodils your favourite, we plant and weep.
Remembrance day, poppies, burial urns.
Nineteen seventy seven, in our sleep.

To have and to hold, to hold and to keep.
The prodigal husband never returns.
Darkness and shadows overwhelmed the deep.

My first home, my next home, the lights retreat.
Remembrance birthday, a red poppy burns.
Nineteen seventy seven, in our sleep.
Darkness and shadows overwhelmed the deep.

Fairy Lights and Holly

Another Christmas coming round the globe.
Another year on earth, we're getting old.
So many pass away, beyond the hill.
We lucky ones should sing and shout: "Here still!"

Our blessings are so numerous, so great.
Around the tree the fairy lights are bright.
And little ones are growing up. Quite soon
they will be walking, running, round the room.

Another Christmas coming to our home,
reminding us of years when we were young.
The tree is evergreen, its leaves like new,
and scented like the forest where it grew.
Around the corner of the year we see
our father, mother. Holly by the tree.

In the Quiet of the Night

The moon is high over Belhaven Bay.
Six swans reflect its silver filaments.
The lapping waves entwined with deep silence
are whispering to them "don't go, please stay".

Six children play, they are picking sea pinks,
and daisy chains are hanging round their necks.
The sun is high, their running joy perfects
a bay of dreams, and forges deeper links.

In cool quiet nights, when wild swans are gathered,
old friends return, like ghosts; the lapping waves
echoing, questioning, things past, things heard.
Familiar forms cast shadows in the caves;
the chains are broken; sing out, sound the gong.
The mute bird spoke, and cried, a last Swan Song.

By Whitberry Point

The ship,
like the wreck in my father's old picture,
patiently waiting,
for the wind to drop.

Ducks bob idly in the February sea.
Smoke billows from a cement factory -
Dunbar's industrial horizon.

The parish church tower is dwarfed.
A horizontal white plume
blows northwards.

To the south, the wind turbines
line up in a row, on the brow of the hill.
Lammermuirs appear a gentle amble,
my vantage point, parallel,
a branch of low growing pine.

Reaching out to the water,
its leaves approach the lapping waves,
the ebb and flow a constant energy,
a melody, in heart's core.

Reverse the years by half a century,
you might glimpse me somewhere here,
hurtling along paths over fallen trees,
on Rowan, our chestnut mare.

To trot through woods was normal then,
to gallop the beaches was grand.
At Belhaven Bay the race horses trained,
but we rode alone on Ravensheugh Sands.

Mirage

The ghostly surface sways.
Is it dancing? Is it whispering?
I see it in the distance,
the past a journey
through forbidden lands.

The Holy Grail beckons,
our quest a common one.
I see Roslyn Chapel from the park below
where Douglas and I walked
a few years ago, or a life-time past.
His kind words, invisible stories,
friendship a raft, to cling to,
linking a departed husband
through intangible threads.
The mud below our feet was real.

Now he has gone,
no longer to be found walking
through Orkney fields,
or telling tales of his youth in Amsterdam,
he has gone to Elysium.

To Edinburgh he returned once more
and in his mother's house
his childhood friends gathered
for a last supper,
he gaunt with cancer.
We spoke of the departed one,
my ghost at the feast,
that one last time.

I hear him still,
weaving the quests of youth,
the defeats of life,
into a tapestry of friendship.
Our paths crossed over decades,
drinking tea or a dram of whisky,
with Rosy, Ellen, Patsy, Charles.

Our arms are linked now,
crossed in a circle,
"Auld Lang Syne" our swansong,
as the dead and the living
meet once more, in a mirage,
that I see on the far horizon.

November Blues

November blue and orange, breakers white
as horses on the sand where paths collide,
and hoof marks trace the arc of luck, and love
is in the wind of this dear beach. I reach
the edge, where water roaring high on waves
bears down and on along the sand. The neighs
of distant animals are lost as drops
of rain mix with the spray, soft on my face.
Yet in the space between the waters sound
I hear in dreams the swimmers, voices found
from deep beneath the ocean; fishes' tails
like mermaids, waving, welcoming. These gales
are glorious, they claim us, own us, now.
Forever, bright November, or January white.

Acknowledgements

With thanks to poets Elspeth Brown and Anna Crowe,
and to songwriters Les Ray and Bil Fulton,
for their friendship and encouragement.

With thanks to Dunbar Writers / Tyne & Esk Writers,
and previously Cambridge Writers,
for their congenial writing contexts.

With thanks to Tyne & Esk Writers for including the poem
"November Blues"
in their collection:
"From the Lighthouse: Poems and Stories from Tyne & Esk Writers",
edited by Claire Askew,
Handsel Press,
Haddington, 2016.

With thanks to Dunbar Writers for including the poem
"Purring at the Moon"
in their collection:
"Wild Words",
by Dunbar Writers Group,
Calder Wood Press,
Dunbar, 2014

With thanks to Bil Fulton
for publishing this first edition under his imprint
BildArt.

INDEX

Lightning Source UK Ltd.
Milton Keynes UK
UKHW020836270520
363959UK00005B/108

9 780995 542037